Living and Learning

LIVING AND LEARNING
Experiences of University after Age 40

Edited by
Judith A Davey, Jenny Neale
and Kay Morris Matthews

VICTORIA UNIVERSITY PRESS

VICTORIA UNIVERSITY PRESS
Victoria University of Wellington
PO Box 600, Wellington

ISBN 0 86473 461 1

First published 2003

National Library of New Zealand Cataloguing-in-Publication Data
Living and learning : experiences of university after age 40 /
edited by Judith A. Davey, Jenny Neale and Kay Morris Matthews.
ISBN 0-86473-461-1
1. Adult college students—New Zealand. 2. Adult education—New Zealand.
3. Education, Higher—New Zealand. I. Davey, Judith A., 1941-
II. Neale, Jenny. III. Morris Matthews, Kay.
378.1982440993—dc 21

Printed by Astra Print, Wellington

CONTENTS

Foreword   7

Acknowledgements   8

Contributors   9

1 Introduction   Judith A Davey   11

2 Early School Leavers   Judith A Davey   25
   and the Path to University

3 Victorious Men –   Jane Renwick   45
   Men Studying Full-Time

4 Older Māori as Students –   Maamari Stephens and   61
   'I'm finally moving from being   Te Ripowai Higgins
   a spectator to being a participant
   in my own culture'

5 Is It Worth It? – Full-Time   Kay Morris Matthews   76
   Teachers Who Study at
   University Part-Time

6 Nurses at University –   Allison Kirkman   93
   Negotiating Academic, Work   and Alison Dixon
   and Personal Pathways

7 'Ageproofing' Your Career –   Deborah Jones and   109
   Age, Gender and the   Sarah Proctor-Thomson
   'New Career'

8 Redundancy as an Opportunity –   Judith A Davey   127
   Job Loss and Education in Midlife

9   University Study in Retirement –   Judith A Davey   146
    Continuity, Substitution and Identity

10 Why Do They Leave? – Mature   Jenny Neale   166
    Students and Withdrawal from Study

11 Conclusion – Common   Judith A Davey, Jenny Neale   178
    Themes and Policy Pointers   and Kay Morris Matthews

Bibliography   189

FOREWORD

I am very pleased to introduce *Living and Learning*, a book arising from research carried out by members of staff at Victoria University of Wellington and linked to the New Zealand Institute for Research on Ageing.

To Benjamin Franklin's comment about the certainty of 'death and taxes', we might also add 'ageing'. These are, of course, related – ageing being the precursor of one and increasingly a drain on the other. It is also an issue which is becoming ever more relevant as the age distribution of our population changes.

As our society changes rapidly in social, technological and economic terms, and as career paths become more volatile, so we become more reliant on continuing education and higher levels of formal qualifications for our employment and financial wellbeing. Typically, about 10% of the students at New Zealand universities are aged over 40 but there is little information from New Zealand about the people who are taking up education opportunities in midlife. We do know that many have to cope with the stresses of studying while in part-time or full-time employment and while dealing with ongoing family commitments. This research seeks to help us better understand the constraints to advanced study in midlife so that we may, as our population ages, help create an educational environment which is suited to the changing needs of our students.

I commend the authors for this timely and important publication. It will do much to help us understand those who will increasingly form a major 'client' group within the higher education sectors in New Zealand and overseas.

Stuart N McCutcheon
Vice Chancellor, Victoria University of Wellington

ACKNOWLEDGEMENTS

The 'Education in Mid and Later Life' research project was initiated by the three editors, with Professor Sikhung Ng of the School of Psychology, Victoria University of Wellington. This group planned and undertook the initial postal survey. The additional contributors joined the research team when in-depth follow-up studies were being undertaken.

Katie Nimmo and Deb Small worked as research assistants for both phases of the project and turned their hands to a variety of tasks and challenges with great efficiency and good humour. Ann Ball and Naomi Trigg assisted with the face-to-face interviewing, Naomi on a voluntary basis. All these people contributed to the success of the project and deserve sincere thanks.

Members of the research group are extremely grateful to everyone who participated in the study and provided information with interest and enthusiasm. Funding for the project was made available through the Strategic Development Fund of Victoria University, the Research Fund of the Faculty of Humanities and Social Sciences and the university's Marketing and Student Affairs Directorate.

CONTRIBUTORS

Judith A Davey is an Associate Professor in the School of Social and Cultural Studies at Victoria University and also Director of the New Zealand Institute for Research on Ageing. Judith's research field is population ageing and its policy implications. This links to her interest in analysing social trends, which has produced five books in the *From Birth to Death* series. Judith has also researched income, transport and housing issues for older people and has published several papers and reports on home equity conversion.

Jenny Neale is the Deputy Dean in the Faculty of Humanities and Social Sciences, and Director of the MA (Applied) in Social Science Research at Victoria University. She has an on-going research interest in higher education. As well as research on the student experience of tertiary education, Jenny is also involved in research on the experience of academics particularly academic women and their careers.

Kay Morris Matthews is an Associate Professor in the School of Education at Victoria University and is the Academic Programme Director of the Gender and Women's Studies programme. An educational historian, Kay has published widely in the fields of girls' and women's education, Māori education and educational policy. Her current research examines gender differences in senior secondary school achievement rates leading to subject choice and participation at university.

Jane Renwick completed her MA (Applied) degree at Victoria University in 2001 and her chapter is derived from her thesis work.

Maamari Stephens was a researcher in Te Kawa a Māui/School of Māori Studies at Victoria University and worked on the 40 plus/30 Tau Neke Atu project.

Te Ripowai Higgins is head of Te Kawa a Māui/School of Māori Studies at Victoria University.

Alison Dixon was the Professor of Nursing at Victoria University and is now the Head of School, Nursing, at Otago Polytechnic.

Allison Kirkman is a senior lecturer in sociology at Victoria University. Her recent publications and research are in the area of gender, health, sexuality and ageing.

Deborah Jones is a Senior Lecturer in Management at Victoria University.

Sarah Proctor-Thomson was formerly a research assistant for The Centre for the Study of Leadership at Victoria University and is now a doctoral student at the Institute for Women's Studies at Lancaster University, England.

1

INTRODUCTION

Judith A Davey

Education, change and ageing

Education is often called upon to help people adapt to social and economic change. Exhortations to encourage continuing or lifelong education and the creation of a 'Learning Society' have come from international organisations including UNESCO, the OECD and national governments across the world, including New Zealand.[1] Peter Jarvis summed up the necessity of lifelong learning if we are to cope successfully –

> The traditional division of life into separate periods – childhood and youth devoted to schooling, adulthood and working life, and retirement – no longer corresponds to things as they are today and corresponds still less to the demands of the future. Today, no one can hope to amass during his or her youth an initial fund of knowledge which will serve for a lifetime. The swift changes taking place in the' world call for knowledge to be continuously updated . . .[2]

Change has been not only swift, but plentiful. Technological change and globalisation have revolutionised everyday life through the use of computers and high-tech communications. Economic restructuring has destabilised labour markets, resulting in unemployment and more volatile careers. Higher levels of education have brought with them credentialism, in which more and higher qualifications are needed to acquire or retain jobs. In the social sphere, changing expectations of male and female roles at home and at work have brought about further change. The 'male breadwinner' concept and traditional family forms are less widespread and gender roles are more complex. We are more aware and more accepting of cultural and lifestyle diversity.

Population ageing adds to the challenge of adaptation. In common with most developed societies, New Zealand is ageing. Half of the population is now over 34 years of age and half will be over 45 by 2051. The effects of ageing are already being felt in the labour market as the large cohort of the 'baby boomers' moves through midlife. Education has been invoked as a response to redundancy and enforced career change, to assist upskilling and combat premature retirement.[3] For people approaching or in retirement – a rapidly growing population group – education is recommended to assist in adjustment to ageing, to provide mental stimulation and resources for new roles – community volunteers, grandparents, carers.[4]

For all these reasons, the topic of education in mid and later life should be of widespread interest – to governments, to educational institutions and to individuals, as they move through life. There is a substantial literature on adult education, examining levels of participation and non-participation, using mainly psychological theories, but also acknowledging contextual factors – external influences, such as work and family situations.[5] Studies of the characteristics of adult learners, disaggregating by demographic and socio-economic characteristics, show many similarities between participants in 'western' countries and over time, for example a decline in participation with age and an increasing interest in adult education by women. Attention has also been paid to special groups, such as women returning to education after child rearing, and to new initiatives in adult education, such as the University of the Third Age.[6] However, there is little information from New Zealand, especially on people who are taking up educational opportunities at university level in midlife. This is the gap which this book seeks to fill.

The 'Education in Mid and Later Life' project

Awareness that New Zealand shares these global social trends and is already experiencing the implications of an ageing population provided the starting point which led to the 'Education in Mid and Later Life' research. If we knew more about the situation of older people who are taking up educational opportunities – their characteristics, motives for participation, the incentives and barriers which they face, their learning experiences and the outcomes – this should throw light on how education might help people plan and manage their futures positively in a rapidly changing society. The findings could also inform the policies of relevant organisations, to achieve the same result.

Why university-level study and why Victoria University? In the absence of other well-developed systems of adult education, the universities play a larger part in New Zealand than in many comparable countries. The sector has undergone very rapid expansion in recent decades.[7] Participation at this level has been strongly encouraged by recent governments, as part of a drive to upskill, mainly motivated by economic considerations. But a special factor is open entry into university in New Zealand by anyone from the age of 21. Eligibility criteria, such as requirements for higher school qualifications, 'foundation' or 'bridge' courses, in countries such as the United Kingdom, set barriers for adults that do not occur in New Zealand universities.

There was a degree of pragmatism in choosing as a case study an organisation where the researchers already worked. We are all familiar with the processes and situation at Victoria University. The university has a total of 15,000 students and offers the full range of academic courses in its faculties of science (including architecture), humanities and social sciences, law and commerce. It provides a very wide and ever-growing range of specialised qualifications, many of them reflecting the capital city status of Wellington, for example in law, commerce and public policy. Victoria is also about average, among New Zealand universities, in the proportion of its students aged 40 and over.[8]

Why age 40? The 'adult' in the literature on adult education is variously defined. Frequently it refers to people aged 21 or 25 and over, as opposed to school leavers in their late teens (sometimes called 'traditional' students). These definitions cover a very wide age range, meaning that adult learners are a diverse, even multigenerational, group in their characteristics, experiences and motivations. Instead, the 'Education in Mid and Later Life' research chose to look at people from age 40 upwards. This range includes people in midcareer as well as those nearing and in retirement. This age group was selected as being old enough to be well beyond 'initial' education (i.e. they are not traditional students), with experience of adult life, families and careers. The younger members are still able to contemplate long-term career development, but are old enough to be vulnerable to change in the labour market.

Research methods

Educational participation in mid and later life is a complex topic and it was therefore appropriate that the original research team was multidisciplinary, incorporating backgrounds in sociology, education, social psychology, and social policy.[9] The methodology was also multidimensional, with several stages to the project –

1a   A demographic analysis of older students in New Zealand educational institutions
1b   Literature Review
2   A postal questionnaire survey of all people aged 40 and over, enrolled at Victoria University in late 1999
3   Nine follow-up studies of specific groups of older students, using face-to-face interviews, telephone interviews and focus group methods.

The postal questionnaire, approved by the appropriate ethics committee, was sent out in early 2000 to 1600 people. It included a mixture of open-ended and precoded questions and covered the circumstances leading to university education, current study experience, educational, family and work backgrounds. Data from 959 respondents (response rate 60%) was coded and analysed. Verbatim comments were also recorded to assist in interpretation and presentation. A full report on the postal survey findings, with a chapter covering the demographic analysis, was published as *Going for it! Older Students at Victoria University* in May 2001.[10] All the respondents who requested feedback were sent an outline of the findings.

The respondents were asked if they were willing to be interviewed in follow-up studies and the response was excellent – 700 people volunteered. This allowed a wider range of in-depth studies than had originally been planned, bringing in new researchers from Māori studies, nursing and midwifery, and management. All the respondents were recontacted and consent gained for the interview stage. Although the nine follow-up studies are all self-contained, all interviewees were asked the 'core' questions and a life course approach was adopted, to put experiences, motivations and outcomes into context.[11] People who could not be interviewed were sent the core questions by mail. More detail on the follow-up studies is included later in this chapter.

Patterns of participation

The Victoria University case study can be placed in a wider national context by examining sources of information on participation in education by people aged 40 and over. Information from the 1996 census suggested that, in the two weeks before the census, about 67,000 people aged 40 and over (5% of the total age group) had been involved in some type of study. At about the same time, there were 13,000 people aged 40-plus enrolled as university students and 14,000 as polytechnic students. Estimates in the non-formal sector are difficult, but possibly another 52,000 had attended community education classes.[12] Information from these sources shows clearly how participation falls with age, so that older people involved in education are highly concentrated in the age group 40 to 59. The 60-plus age group is significantly under-represented in formal tertiary study. All the sources show that about two-thirds of the group involved in education are female, even though women make up just over half of the 40-plus population. However, male/female proportions among older students become closer with advancing age and are much closer for full-time study.

The ethnic breakdown of people 40 and over involved in education follows population patterns in that Pākehā (New Zealanders of European descent) are the majority (83% of university and 80% of polytechnic students in the age group). However, Māori and Asians have significant representation. Pacific Islanders on the other hand tend to be under-represented in most of the data sets. Women outnumber men in all ethnic groups.

The 40-plus group, both males and females, have lower levels of participation in education than the total adult population and are less likely to be studying for a qualification than younger people. The 1996 census information showed that 10% of total adults had been studying, but only 5% of those 40 and over.[13] Although the numbers of people who had been studying grew between 1991 and 1996, this did not keep pace with growth in the age group 40 and over, as the baby boom bulge began to come through. So participation rates appear to be static. Table 1.1 shows the figure for universities and polytechnics.

Table 1.1: Rates of participation in education for the 40-plus population
and total adults (percentage of groups who had participated in education)

Data source	Coverage	Males 40-plus	Total males	Females 40-plus	Total females	Total 40-plus	Total
University	1991	0.8	3.4	1.3	3.4	1.1	3.4
	1996	0.8	3.6	1.2	3.9	1.0	3.8
Polytechnic	1991	0.8	3.0	0.8	2.4	0.8	2.7
	1996	0.9	3.4	1.2	3.5	1.1	3.4

In summary (based mainly on census data), people age 40 and over who participate in education in New Zealand have the following characteristics –
- two-thirds are women
- three-quarters study part-time
- nearly half are women studying part-time
- four out of five are aged 40 to 59
- only one in 20 is aged 60 or more.

Findings from the Victoria University survey

Personal characteristics
Overall, the personal characteristics of the Victoria University respondents made them similar to the national pattern already outlined. They were also representative of Victoria students aged 40 and over, as a whole.
- Seventy percent were female. This corresponds to 56% female for the total Victoria student body in 1999.
- Two out of three were in the 40–49 age group; 29% were aged 50–59 and 5% 60 and over.
- Māori (including Māori/Pākehā) made up 8%, with Pacific Islanders making up 3% and Asian 5%. This leaves 83% Pākehā or other ethnicity.

Four out of five respondents had family members who had been to university, but this was more likely to be their siblings or children than their parents. Most had higher school qualifications – sixth form certificate or above. Only 8% left with no school qualifications. Following on from this, only 7.5% had no further formal education or training beyond secondary school. One in five already had an undergraduate degree before they began their current period of study at Victoria University and one in ten already had a postgraduate degree. A considerable proportion also had teaching or nursing qualifications.

Study patterns

- A quarter of respondents were full-time students. This is much lower than the 60% figure for all Victoria students.
- Students who responded to our survey were heavily concentrated in the faculty of humanities and social sciences – 65% (total student figures in brackets – 47%). Next came commerce – 22% (20%), then law – 7% (12%) and finally science, including architecture – 6% (21%).
- Older students are much more likely to be studying for post-graduate qualifications than the student body as a whole – 35% were doing Master's courses (all students 9%). Certificate courses were also popular – 17% (4% of all students).

Respondents to the postal survey were working on 67 different qualifications, of which the most popular was the BA – 17.5%. There was a similar variety among the subjects studied – 75 in all. Education was by far the most popular subject, followed by nursing and midwifery, and law.

At home and at work

While they were enrolled as students at Victoria University in 1999, 53% of respondents were also working full-time (30 hours and over) and 20% worked part-time. Overall four out of five were in some kind of paid work. Of those who were employed, the vast majority were in either professional/technical occupations – 72% – or in the managerial/administration category – 16%.

Seventy percent of respondents lived with a partner, either married or de facto, and a further 5% had a partner whom they did not live with. This leaves 25% unpartnered. The pattern is close to 'social' marital status patterns for the age group recorded in the 1996 census. The respondents' household composition pattern was also close to census figures – 43% lived with a partner and children; 22% with a spouse/partner only, and 16% lived alone.

Although the personal incomes of the respondents were spread over the range from $10,000 or less per annum to $70,000-plus, they mostly lived in high-income households. Sixty-one percent had household incomes over $50,000 per annum and 44% over $70,000.

Motives and decisions
Most of the respondents – nearly 85% – discussed their intention to return to study with other people, especially their spouse and/or children. Three out of every four received backing for the decision; 13% reported a mixed reaction and only 6% said that their nearest and dearest did not support their intention to study. Roughly two-thirds of the respondents said that they had faced difficulties in returning to education. These mainly took the form of work-related demands and family commitments. At the university end the main difficulty was cost. Some noted more personal difficulties, such as lack of self-confidence and study skills.

The main motivations for study were either work related – wishing to acquire new knowledge or qualifications to improve job performance and prospects – or personal development and fulfillment. Many respondents did not experience a specific 'trigger' event which prompted them to go to university. Where they did, this was most likely to be reduced demands for childcare (for women), job loss or redundancy (for men) and the money becoming available (often through employers).

University experience
There were high levels of satisfaction with most aspects of university experience covered in the questionnaire, especially with the choice of courses. People were most dissatisfied with contact with other students and their own academic performance. Most respondents had faced barriers in achieving their aims at university, and these came in many forms. The most common were time demands made by work and family commitments. Financial problems and cost in general were also important. Some people mentioned difficulty with study skills, energy and motivation. A few suggested aspects of course arrangements or teaching at Victoria University. In both levels of satisfaction and levels of difficulty faced, the Pacific Island group stood out as being less positive about their university experience.

Despite cost being cited as a barrier, 43% of respondents did not answer the question on financial difficulties and 17% said they had none. The rest raised a great variety of issues – loss of disposable income, high course costs, reluctance to incur debt, problems with the student loan scheme and the need to meet family expenses. Some had children who needed funding for their tertiary studies at the same time as their parent.

Most respondents funded their studies from multiple sources – only 30% from a single source. Half had income from full-time work and 30% from part-time work (sometimes both over the course of several years' study); 23% had a student loan, but only 9% a student allowance. About the same proportion had received income from a welfare benefit. More important than public sector funding was family support (mentioned by 32%) and personal or family savings (mentioned by 27%). Employers provided funding for 26% of respondents. Other sources mentioned included grants or scholarships and superannuation – government or occupational.

The most important incentive to achieve their study aims – mentioned by one-third of the respondents – was internal motivation and striving for personal development. Other incentives were the goal of achieving a qualification, support of family and friends and of university staff and the desire not to waste their financial investment in education. The vast majority (88%) of respondents thought there was some advantage in being a student aged 40 and over. This was mainly because of greater life and work experience, more motivation and focus, and a higher degree of confidence and maturity. But there were also disadvantages, mentioned by 74%. The most frequently mentioned disadvantages concerned the greater commitments to family and work required of older people and a general shortage of time. Some mentioned greater difficulty in learning and less effective memory. Some also talked about difficulties in relating to younger students.

Respondents were asked what advice they would give to people 40 and over who were contemplating study at university. There was a wide variety of responses, but over a third (38%) gave unqualified encouragement to 'Go for it!'. Most of the advice was about study and study habits, with less said about how to handle work and family matters. Prospective older students were encouraged to be organised and focused, to manage their time well, not be afraid to ask for help, to use support systems and to choose their courses carefully.

The future
The vast majority of respondents considered that gaining a Victoria University qualification would benefit them in future – 78% thought that it would have a positive effect on their paid work and career prospects, 62% thought the same about their future study intentions. People had more neutral views about the effect their qualification would have on their social lives or community involvement.

Comparisons
Compared to the New Zealand population aged 40 and over, the respondents to the postal survey were younger, more highly qualified, higher in the socio-economic scale and had higher income levels. They were, however, similar in their ethnic make-up and household circumstances and typical of people 40-plus who are involved in education. Compared to the Victoria University student body as a whole, the respondents were more predominantly female, highly concentrated in the faculty of humanities and social sciences and much more likely to be studying part-time and at postgraduate level.

There were, however, differences within the respondent group based on age, gender and ethnicity. For example, younger respondents were more preoccupied with paid work and family compared to people aged 60 and over. There were differences in funding sources between men and women, with men more likely to have income from paid work. Māori and Pacific Island students were more likely to be studying at undergraduate level and studying full-time than people in other ethnic groups. These differences suggested that in-depth study of specific groups of older students would highlight special characteristics and circumstances, and allow a deeper analysis of issues related to education in mid and later life.

Outline of the following chapters

Each of the nine follow-up studies occupies a chapter in this book. They draw on a common source of data, and are based on a life course framework, showing how education fits into adult life and is influenced by earlier experiences. All bring the respondents to life through the use of verbatim quotes, vignettes and the use of personal pseudonyms. But at the same time, the studies highlight a great diversity of experience among older university students and differences in the challenges which they face.

In chapter two, Judith Davey looks at an atypical group of older students. The literature suggests that initial school experiences have a determining influence on later educational involvement, yet one in six of the 40-plus students at Victoria University left school with less than four years of secondary education. How did these people find themselves at university after the age of 40? An analysis of their experiences suggests how others may be helped, in the interests of equity, so that early school leavers are not left behind in the rising tide of credentialism.

While there is a considerable amount of research on older women returning to education, and how they juggle the commitments of study with the responsibilities of caring for their families, there are few studies that focus on men. In chapter three, Jane Renwick draws on case studies of men aged 40–59 who were full-time students at Victoria University and who had moved from the role of full-time worker (and possibly family breadwinner) to that of full-time student.

The postal survey suggested that Māori students, as a whole, have different experiences in tertiary education than their non-Māori counterparts. Older Māori students find themselves faced with a special irony. Often denied the chance to learn about their heritage in earlier years, such students now find themselves at an essentially Pākehā tertiary institution to learn their tikanga and reo Māori. Interviews with mature Māori students from areas such as law, education and Māori studies, analysed by Maamari Stephens and Te Ripowai Higgins, and presented in chapter four, reveal how older Māori students experience this redis-covery of their culture and language.

People with teaching qualifications were well represented in the Victoria University survey and education is a very popular subject for older students. This is because policy in New Zealand has encouraged teachers to enroll for degree study as part of their professional development. From a compilation of educational and career profiles, Kay Morris Matthews highlights the motives and experiences of teachers who took up part-time university study while also employed in full-time teaching (chapter five). This entailed personal, financial, work-related and institutional pressures. How will their newly completed qualifications affect their career paths?

There are parallels between the chapter five on teachers and chapter six which looks at women who were already qualified and working as nurses or midwives when they entered university. Allison Kirkman and Alison Dixon found several types of motivation in this group. For some, postgraduate studies were essential for their career development in all areas of practice. For others, it was an opportunity to pursue academic studies other than nursing and midwifery and perhaps a change in career direction. Another motive was the chance to broaden their education once their families were more independent.

Chapter seven continues to explore links between work and education in midlife. Management is not usually a career that women have dreamed of from an early age and worked deliberately towards. Deborah Jones and Sarah Proctor-Thomson interviewed women management students who 'ended up' as managers. Rather than opening doors to a new career or teaching new skills, management education later in life has been, for them, a way of legitimising their identities as successful middle and senior managers and confirming a set of capabilities that they have already achieved.

Losing a job in midlife can be an unsettling experience at best and often a catastrophe, especially given the reality of age discrimination in the labour market. In chapter eight, Judith Davey shows that it can also be a trigger for further educational involvement. As well as gathering information on the working, family and educational lives of this group, the interviews with respondents who had experienced redundancy focused on the experience and outcomes of job loss and how these were linked to recent study at Victoria University. The findings show that redundancy can, in fact, be an opportunity – for re-evaluation and life change.

The motive for university study from age 60 onwards is likely to be self-fulfillment and personal development rather than job prospects, but is nonetheless valuable if it contributes to positive or successful ageing. This was certainly the case for the older students interviewed by Judith Davey. The interviews, which form the basis for chapter nine, explored what education had meant to the group through the whole of their lives, illustrating patterns of continuity and discontinuity. They also showed how education can substitute for paid work and contribute to the preservation of self-esteem in later life. This contrasts with the vocational motivations of younger interviewees.

A great deal of effort goes into recruiting students to tertiary study but then little emphasis is placed on retention. Why do older students leave? In chapter ten, Jenny Neale explores the reasons why students aged 40 and over do not stay and complete their qualifications. Their experiences are compared with those of younger students at Victoria University. Common issues include money, motivation, time and balancing study with home and work responsibilities, highlighting the areas that mature students find most difficult when taking up study at this stage of their life.

The final chapter brings together some common threads, illustrating what our findings show about the significance of university education for people aged 40 and over. The discussion raises issues for older students and for people who may be contemplating study in mid and later life. More broadly, it draws conclusions for universities, and the tertiary sector as a whole, and outlines implications for policy on lifelong education. Thus, our conclusions relate back to issues raised in the introduction on the significance of lifelong education and how it may be promoted as a way of assisting people to cope in an ageing and changing society.

Notes

1   Faure et al (1972), Delors (1996), Tight (1996), Belanger and Valdivielso (1997), Elliott (1999). In New Zealand, The Tertiary Education Advisory Commission (TEAC) adopted 'Life Long Learning for a Knowledge Society' as a slogan and endorsed the principle of lifelong learning in its Initial Report – *Shaping a Shared Vision*. Wellington, July 2000. www.teac.govt.nz. Accessed 1.12.01.

2   Jarvis (1997) p.99.

3   Cabinet Office (2000).

4   Withnall (1994), Schuller (1993), Walker (1996), Midwinter (1998).

5   The literature on adult participation in education explores many relevant psychological and personality factors. Reviewed by Cross (1981), Woodley (1987), Yang (1998), McGivney (1993), Henry and Basile (1994). But the research agenda has been widened to acknowledge the importance of social influences – both personal and contextual. (Gooderham (1993)).

6   The adult education literature and that specific to New Zealand, is concerned mainly with participation and non-participation (Boshier (1970), (1971), Benseman (1992), Tobias (1991), Taylor (1995)) and issues related to history, policy and the supply of services (Hindmarsh and Davies (1995), Methven and Hansen (1996), Benseman et al. (1996), Tobias (1998)). There are several small scale studies of adults (frequently defined as ages 21 or 25 plus) at universities, some looking especially at women's experiences (Knight and Hitchman (1988), Miller (1993), Morrison (1995), Reeder (1997), Ash (1999)). University of the Third Age (U3A) in New Zealand has been studied by Battersby (1985), Heppner (1994) and Swindell (1999).

7   There were 11,000 university students in New Zealand in 1951 and 88,000 in 1991, an increase of 700% (Official Yearbook figures).

8   People aged 40 and over represented 10.4% of the total Victoria University student body in 1999 and 13% in 2000, according to university records. A comparison can be made with other New Zealand universities using information from the New Zealand Vice-Chancellors' Committee (NZVCC) University Graduate Destinations Surveys. Figures for completed university qualifications can be used as a proxy for participation in education at this level. In 1998 Massey had the highest figures for graduates aged 40 and over – 25% (related to the provision of distance education), followed by Waikato – 15%. Auckland, Victoria and Otago Universities all had around 10%, with lower figures for Canterbury and Lincoln (NZVCC (1999)). Victoria's figure is therefore close to the average.

9   Biographical information about the original research team and the authors of the present volume is included in the Acknowledgements and Contibutors pages.

10 Davey (2001). Several conference and journal papers have also been based on the postal questionnaire (and follow-up studies) findings.

11 Following West (1995) and Farnes (1996).

12 Ministry of Education estimate, 1995.

13 For total males the figure was 8.5% and for total females 11%, but for the 40-plus group the respective figures were 4% for males and 6% for females. Participation rates for the total population appear to have grown between 1991 and 1996, but were static for the 40-plus population.

2

EARLY SCHOOL LEAVERS AND THE PATH TO UNIVERSITY

Judith A Davey

An atypical group of older students

One in every six of the 40-plus students at Victoria University were classified as 'early school leavers' meaning that they left school with less than four years of secondary education, on or soon after their 15th birthday, which marked the end of compulsory schooling. This was an extremely common pattern up to the 1970s. In 1950, 75% of young people left New Zealand schools with less than four years of secondary education. The 1960 figure was 70%, but this fell to 51% in 1970 and to 39% in 1980.[1] People who were 40 at the time of the Victoria University survey were 15 in 1975 and those who were 60 reached school-leaving age in 1955.

In the period in question, young people left school early for a range of reasons, and these will be illustrated by the experiences of people interviewed in the 'Education in Mid and Later Life' research. How they felt about their school experience was one of the 'push' factors. Compared to total survey respondents, more early school leavers said they did not like school – 31% as against 19%

The 'pull' factors included the easy availability of employment as the New Zealand economy flourished up to the 1970s. But social expectations and attitudes towards education were also important, including experience of university in the family of origin. A high proportion of the early leavers group had family members who had attended university – 74% as against 80% of total survey respondents. However, this was unlikely to be parents or siblings. Instead, a higher proportion of their children had been to university – 49% (39% of total respondents) and also 'other' family members, including grandchildren, nieces and nephews – 28% (14% of total respondents). The role of younger family members in encouraging university study by their elders may therefore be significant.

School Certificate[2] examinations take place in the fifth form and when most of the 40-plus students were at school, to 'pass' School Certificate required reaching the prescribed standard of marks over several subjects. This made the exams much more of a challenge than today, when single subject passes are possible. Hence 42% of the 155 people classified as early school leavers left school with no qualifications and 58% with School Certificate only.

These patterns make the early school leavers group atypical among older students at Victoria University, and generally. Only 8% of total respondents left with no school qualifications and 17% with School Certificate only. The vast majority gained higher school qualifications – Sixth Form Certificate, University Entrance, Scholarship or Bursary. Lack of higher school qualifications did not, however, prevent the early school leavers group from achieving university education later in life, as this chapter will show.[3] Their experience challenges theories which suggest that initial educational achievement largely determines later and lifelong participation.

Characteristics of the early school leavers group

The early school leavers were similar to total Victoria students aged 40-plus in their gender and age structure and there were few differences in household circumstances. However, the group had a higher representation of Māori and Pacific Islanders – 21% as against 9% overall. This corresponds to generally lower levels of educational attainment in these ethnic groups, especially in the age range under consideration.

Early school leavers appeared in all the socio-economic categories, defined on an occupational basis. But they were under-represented in the 'higher' levels – 56% were classified as professional/technical or managerial/administrative as against 73% of total respondents – and over-represented among unemployed people and the non-labour force groups (early school leavers 23%, total respondents 16%). Both groups are, nevertheless, of high socio-economic status compared to the New Zealand population as a whole. Similarly, early school leavers had a range of incomes, but were concentrated in the lower levels – 43% had

Table 2.1: Tertiary qualifications – early school leavers and total respondents

	Early school leavers %	Total respondents %
Nursing/Teaching/Police qualifications	20	24
Undergraduate degree	16	26
Postgraduate degrees and certificates/diplomas	2	15
Other certificates/diplomas	37	20
Other, unclear or no reply	5	7
No further educational qualifications	20	8
	100	100

Note: Figures include partly completed qualifications in each category.

annual household incomes of $40,000 or less as against 28% of total respondents.

Most early school leavers had undertaken some further education and training despite having less than four years of secondary schooling. Only 20% had no tertiary qualifications on entering Victoria University for their current period of study. Compared to the survey respondents as a whole, fewer had gained degrees, but a higher percentage had some type of vocational certificate (Table 2.1).

These characteristics make early school leavers atypical, but of especial interest. What factors led to their leaving school early and what happened next? How were their family lives interrelated with paid work and further educational opportunities and what eventually led them, after the age of 40, to study at university? Having outlined the main characteristics of the group as a whole, we now focus in depth on the stories of a selection of early school leavers, told through personal interviews.

Twenty women and seven men were interviewed in the follow-up to the postal survey. They represented 17% of the 155 early school leavers, with about the same proportion male and female. The average age of the interviewees was 54. They included people from several ethnic groups, but ethnicity is not mentioned further in this discussion, to preserve confidentiality.

Families of origin

At the time when the early school leaver interviewees (described from here on as early school leavers) were born, their mothers were predominantly housewives, as was usually the case then for married women with children. Where their mothers had paid work this was likely to be unskilled. Several mothers had been shop assistants, two had worked in businesses run by their husbands. Other occupations included tea lady, cook and barmaid. Only four early school leavers had mothers with occupations slightly higher in the socio-economic scale – one was a nurse, one a post office worker, one a pay clerk and one a secretary. None had university-level education.

There was a wide range of occupations for the group's fathers. Eleven were clearly working class – railway workers, labourers, a freezing worker, boilermaker, truck driver and mechanic. Seven were in commercial occupations including retail trade and small business and one was a farmer. Five were in public sector work, often difficult to categorise by class, including two in the armed forces and two post office workers. One father could be classified as a professional – a cost accountant. Only two interviewees reported that their fathers had university experience.

Leaving school

The early school leavers in the study were in secondary school in the 1970s or before, when compulsory education ended at age 15, and a high proportion of boys and girls left with less than four years at secondary school. None of the people interviewed left school with qualifications which would have qualified them to progress to university.

There were mixed views as the interviewees looked back at their school days. Some failed School Certificate and didn't even think about university at the time. Others had ambitions to continue their education, but were prevented by their home circumstances. Teenage rebellion, related to peer pressure, turned many off school, especially when discipline was strict. Carla 'got in a group' misbehaved and 'dumbed down'. Peter and Alan described themselves as headstrong, rebellious and resentful students. Some rebelled against parents as well as school. Celia deliberately didn't work at school so her parents would be forced into letting her leave.

As a result of such behaviour and attitudes, several people (along with many other adolescents) did not get on well with their teachers. This may have been another factor leading to early leaving. Rose and Elsbeth were at catholic girls schools. Both wanted to go to university, but felt rejected and disliked by their teachers. Elsbeth was outgoing, garrulous and independent, full of stories about travelling the world with her parents. But the teachers said she was a show-off and a liar and made other people jealous. Rose was a bright 'scholarship' girl, but because her mother was a poor widow she received no encouragement and was told she should leave and earn some money.

Dissuasion was, however, more likely to come from home than from school, especially for the girls. Sometimes this was not active discouragement, but a failure to support further education by parents who were struggling financially. Katherine had to leave when her brother started secondary school because her parents couldn't afford to support two children. Sam thought that leaving school would help the family finances. The normal and expected working class ethos for both boys and girls was to get a job as soon as possible and contribute money to the family.

> Nothing in the local culture suggested any other option. An older brother stayed until age 16 and this was considered unusual. (Geraldine)

> It was assumed that you left school at 15 and if you did well you got an apprenticeship. (Alan)

This attitude was not confined to the working class. Eileen came from a farming family with no expectation that young people would go to university. It was presumed that Richard would join the family's business. Sara's widowed mother was a successful retailer, who didn't value education because she had been successful through hard work. So university was never suggested, even though the family was by then financially comfortable.

While the necessity to work and to earn applied equally to boys and girls, parental attitudes to education were influenced by gender expectations. It was assumed that girls would soon marry and that their working lives would be short. Deborah's family saw her as a farmer's wife. There was no necessity for her head to be 'filled full of nonsense'.

Ruth's domineering father found his daughter a job in a local bank and directed her to leave school.

> He wasn't particularly mean – his attitude was normal at the time. (Ruth)

Moving into paid work

Given their youth and lack of qualifications, the early school leavers moved into basic grade jobs. Sometimes parents, especially fathers, found work for their children, as in Ruth's case. Sam and Carla worked in the same factories as their fathers. Most of the girls went into clerical (office juniors), typing or related work. The exceptions were Barbara and Louise who took up retail work. Rachel became a trainee draftswoman. For working class girls an office job was considered superior to shop or factory work and could lead to advancement. Moira was 'sent to Gilbey's to learn how to type' and Sara received training on a Burroughs accounting machine.

Young men were much more likely to move from school into formal apprenticeships. Alan, Stan and Rex became apprentices in various branches of engineering, and Richard began training in the family business. The other four men in the group moved into unskilled labouring work.

In the 1950s and 60s jobs were plentiful and could be changed at will. Many interviewees had several jobs in quick succession, but were frequently bored and unchallenged. Their restlessness also arose from a desire to leave home and sometimes to travel in the time-honoured way for young New Zealanders. Deborah was especially keen on travelling even while she was at school –

> In detentions I used to read the *National Geographic* [magazine] and I left school with a burning desire to travel. I was doing clerical work for the Post Office and was asked to join the pension plan. This interfered with my savings for travel so I left.

The young women often travelled further afield than the men. Stan's 'OE' (overseas experience) was around the North Island and Len had a year in Australia. However, the men were more willing to elaborate on their footloose and irresponsible youthful lifestyle, reflecting greater freedom given to males at the time. Rex abandoned his apprenticeship for the 'joys of alcohol, drugs and the big city life' (of Auckland). Peter drove his car too fast and chased girls. Len saw himself as another James Dean with motorbike and rebellious attitude.

At the same time, about a quarter of the early school leavers were keeping in touch with education. Apprenticeships required some study and several women also did shorthand-typing courses at night school. Alan did trade training at a polytechnic and became a junior technical manager in a manufacturing firm. After four years as a builder's labourer, Peter thought he 'had better do something'. He took some management courses and moved on to become a sales representative.

Forming a family

For most of the early leavers group, marriage was the next step, sometimes following hard on the heels of leaving school and starting work. To marry and have children young was very much the expectation in the 1950s and 60s. All of the group married, apart from four of the women, and almost all did so before the age of 25, many at 18 or 19. Three women admitted they were pregnant at marriage, but others may have been. Indra (now aged 52) was 'sent to the country' when she became pregnant at 18, again a common occurrence at the time. She was going to have her baby adopted, but her mother persuaded the father to marry Indra three weeks after the birth 'to save face'. The marriage lasted only a few months.

Childbearing followed very quickly after marriage. All those who married had children, but their families were generally smaller than their families of origin. In some cases the women stopped work when they had children, but others continued, usually part-time and intermittently. Families moved around the country following the male breadwinner's career, which meant that wives had to pursue their careers as best they could. The type of work they had experience of was available almost everywhere, even if advancement was limited. For some of the group movement was international. Betty, Geraldine and Alan emigrated from Britain to New Zealand with their newly married spouses. Others took off from New Zealand to live in other parts of the world for a while.

Work, learning and family life

As young adults the lives of the early school leavers group, especially those who had children, were dominated by the competing demands of paid and unpaid work. Education, whether formal or informal, was another important influence, intersecting with career and family, sometimes with considerable difficulty.

Several people attempted to compensate for their lack of school qualifications by taking School Certificate or University Entrance at a later stage. Often, for the women, attempts to advance their education were brought to a halt by marriage and motherhood. Louise and Celia tried to study by correspondence but neither found this successful. For the men, supporting a family and sometimes doing work on the home were preoccupations. Stan started studying for an engineering certificate, but didn't finish it. He was too busy with building a house, his work and his five children. To compensate people who helped with the house, he spent extra time fixing their cars. Len also wanted to study engineering, but needed to take School Certificate English and maths three times a week at night school. He found this too hard and failed the exams.

Other interviewees took up job-oriented education, again with varying degrees of success. Sometimes this was related to their first job, but more often, educational opportunities followed a change of career direction. Alan had been working as a TV technician after emigrating to New Zealand, but was bored with it. He had been a union representative and when he was approached to work full-time for a union he took the opportunity. He was doing research and quasi-legal work and, with the encouragement of his employer, he began a law degree. Sam was working for the railways when a priest recruited him as a parish worker and he was sent overseas on a three-month course.

Sometimes it was a hobby which encouraged learning, especially an interest in art. Moira did evening art classes and was able to earn some money from her work. At age 35 she did University Entrance through correspondence and later bursary-level art at school. Deirdre was also interested in drawing. She took private art tuition while at home with children, but dropped out as her family grew.

My teacher said I was too married to be a serious artist.

These interests were not confined to women. Richard described himself as 'not academically minded' and work in the family business was very time consuming as he advanced up the management ladder. But as his children grew and achieved in their education he felt he was stagnating and wanted to 'improve himself'. He took some night classes, but these did not lead to qualifications. Peter had moved on from being a sales representative to work as a meat inspector. When he was about 30 he started university-level distance courses in psychology and philosophy for interest. In the off season for the meatworks he didn't have a lot to do and used the time for reading.

Access to education could be problematic. When Cynthia's three children were young she helped at Playcentre and did the supervisor's course. It was only when she and her husband moved to Wellington that she was able to train in kindergarten teaching. Len also had no access to architecture courses in the two provincial centres where he lived for several years.

Others had no involvement in education in their early adult life. Ruth married at 19 and devoted herself to her husband and family – 'a dutiful wife for 27 years' – before she walked out in her late forties. Barbara also married early and worked with her husband on their farm.

Deborah was the only member of the early school leavers group to attempt university-level courses before the age of 30. At age 22 she took off for London. A 'patronising boyfriend' pushed her to go to university, so she attended night school to get the required 'A' levels. At 25 she went to the London School of Economics but didn't finish her degree at that stage.

For all of the other women who had families, marriage and childbearing came before tertiary study. Among the women, Indra and Carla were unusual in beginning their BAs while their children were still young. Both found study valuable in getting through those difficult years and involvement in early childhood education was influential in their decision to continue their own studies. Indra was raising two children on her own in her late thirties. She started a BA in education and psychology – 'it was a good move for me'. Carla had her first child at 21 and by 30 was a solo mother of two living on a welfare benefit. She decided to study literature –

I wanted to prove something to myself, to articulate my ideas to myself and other people – it didn't matter how long it took. Some people said discouraging things, but they didn't have any effect. I studied for pleasure. Study was my release, my sanity saver, my social life for ten years.

The only male interviewee to begin university study before the age of 40 was Alan, by then a trade union official. He had been against university study – what he called 'working class abhorrence' – but changed his mind. His second wife, who was 'a long-standing student' managed to start him in a university class by registering both of them and then withdrawing herself. Alan found he actually enjoyed studying and took more courses in Māori and anthropology before embarking on a law degree. As already noted, several interviewees tried distance study but in general they did not like it because of the isolation. Only Cynthia managed to complete a full degree extramurally.

Study at Victoria University

For most of the early school leavers, their recent experience at Victoria University was their first taste of tertiary study (leaving aside distance education). Despite low levels of school attainment, information from the postal survey showed that early school leavers were in all levels of study at Victoria University, but over half were undergraduates (Table 2.2). They were represented in all faculties, but nearly three-quarters were in the faculty of humanities and social sciences as against 63% of total survey respondents. And a higher proportion was studying full-time – a third as opposed to a quarter of total respondents.

Table 2.2: Level of study – early school leavers and total respondents

	Early school leavers %	Total respondents %
Undergraduate degree or certificate	51	37
Postgraduate Diploma/Certificate or Honours	9	15
Master's or MA Applied	30	35
Doctorate	4	7
COP*	6	6
	100	100

* Certificate of Proficiency, a course by course approach

The early school leavers group were working on 28 different qualifications and 39 subject majors. A quarter were registered for BA (total respondents 18%) and 8% for BEd (total respondents 3%). The top ranking subjects for the group were similar to overall patterns, led by nursing, education and law, but English ranked higher for those who had left school early. The study of English language and literature is a traditional avenue for older students to approach university study. The people who were interviewed followed this pattern – their most popular subjects being art history, English literature, education and political science. Several were taking law and commerce subjects, often in combination with others. None were studying physical or biological sciences, mathematics or computer science.

Why study? – Motivations for educational involvement in adulthood

In the postal survey, respondents were asked to rank factors which motivated their study at Victoria University. The male early school leavers produced similar patterns to total male survey respondents with respect to work-related and personal development motives (Table 2.3).[4] However, the women were more likely to place personal development first and less likely to choose work-related motives, compared to their female counterparts in the full survey. This is possibly because gender-related factors prevented them from expressing their educational aspirations earlier. Early school leavers were also more likely to suggest that setting an example to children and grandchildren was a motive for their participation.

Table 2.3: Motivations for educational involvement – percentage ranking the motivation first

	Males		Females	
	ESL group	Total respondents	ESL group	Total respondents
Work related	59	56	53	60
Personal development	45	47	60	45
Setting an example	6	2	12	5

In some cases early school leavers came to university study with motives clearly related to their current job. These can be illustrated by the experiences of Celia and Barbara.

Celia had never married and had no children. Her early adult life had been spent in a variety of jobs, interspersed with periods of illness and unemployment. When she was 27 she went overseas and began teaching English. Returning to New Zealand, Celia tried to reskill by taking a course in electronic engineering, but afterwards could not find a job. After another period of teaching in Asia, Celia returned to work in another language school, feeling exploited and undervalued. She was made redundant (for the second time). Soon afterwards, encouraged by an employer, she enrolled in a diploma course for teaching English as a second language, hoping that this qualification would give her respect and proper pay for the work she had been doing.

Barbara was widowed in her thirties. With her two children she moved to the city when it became obvious she could not manage the farm on her own. She worked first as a nanny and then in a childcare centre. She could see the difference between herself and the trained staff in how they related to the children. There was some pressure to train from her employers, but she could see that it was also a mark of confidence, so she began to study part-time for a Bachelor of Education degree. It was hard work, because of her lack of educational experience, as well as a financial and physical strain.

Sometimes people took up study at Victoria University to assist a change of career (or to establish a clear career path) in the same way as other early school leavers had done earlier in their lives.

Louise had considerable difficulties in her marriage and was working as a teacher's aide. She consulted a business psychologist about career development and was advised to do a degree. She took a BA in sociology and psychology because of her interest in working with people.

While working as a carpenter and coping with unemployment and a large family, Len was encouraged to try his hand at drafting by an architect who gave him some informal training. He developed an interest in architecture but was not able to think about training until he moved to Wellington. At the same time he developed an illness which made it impossible for him to continue in manual work. Even though he recognised that he had not done well at school, he thought he could manage university study because of his enthusiasm for architecture and his keenness on reading.

There is an intermediate category between work-related and personal development motives. These are examples where work-related factors were relevant in the choices made, but personal interest was their main motivation.

Cynthia had built on her Playcentre and kindergarten training to become an early childhood education advisor – acquiring a degree by distance study. Later she was tutoring in a polytechnic and her employers suggested further study. She decided not to continue in her professional area, instead beginning a Master's course in an area of recreational studies where she had long-term interests.

Katherine had been a typist, but worked her way up to become a political speechwriter. When she was in her early fifties and working as a polytechnic tutor in secretarial studies she needed a tertiary qualification. Despite her lack of a degree she was accepted for an MBA course and passed with distinction. After this Katherine began to suffer from an illness which made regular work impossible and, because of her political experience, she was invited to do a PhD in political studies.

Just under half of the early school leavers could be classified as having work-related motives for their study at Victoria University. Thus a slight majority were studying for personal development and fulfilment. But this group can also be subdivided. In some cases, the interviewees expressed long-term aspirations for education or specifically for university study.

Elsbeth had mostly been in clerical work, but she had taken courses in English literature, counselling and naturopathy and wanted to develop these interests. She had had more than her share of family trauma. Her husband was controlling and obsessive, objecting both when she wanted to study and also when she went out to work. When Elsbeth was 52 her marriage finally broke up and this was followed by the death of her father, a suicide in the family and her own ill-health. Eventually she managed to attend a 'Going Back to Study' course. This gave her the confidence to begin full-time study for a BA, choosing education and social policy to develop her interests in human development and social justice.

Several people expressed their motivation as 'love of learning'.

Geraldine spent most of her life as a secretary, but was always interested in learning. She took a job at a university to see what it was all about and found that she was 'just as clever' as the students. At the age of 40 she began part-time study for a BA, following this with an honours degree, a teaching diploma and an MA before embarking on PhD study in philosophy – a 'deeply rooted' interest of hers.

At age 37, Rose was in Australia. Her three children were at school and she was doing part-time clerical work. Encouraged by her employers, she did two years study towards her BA before the family moved on to New Zealand. She completed her degree in her fifties. After retirement she continued into an honours degree. She said she had 'a lifelong love of study and getting to know things – English literature was always my thing'.

Another aspect of study for personal development was the desire which some of the early school leavers had to do something different, something just 'for themselves'.

Eileen had no children and lived alone. Although she had done no study since leaving school, she had become an office administrator and was financially secure. However she felt that she had 'outgrown' her job. Following the deaths of her parents and her only brother, and encouraged by her work colleagues and friends (all of whom had professional training), she felt that 'time was right' to do something different. At the age of 44 she took on full-time study for a BA in political science, because her family had always been interested in this area.

By the time he was in his fifties, Richard found that his workload was decreasing and his children were at university. Inspired by their example he decided it was his turn to do something for himself – perhaps 'a little bit selfishly' he thought. He had no specific subject in mind, but took on a BA programme in European languages and English literature.

The outcomes and value of university education for early school leavers

Leaving school early and moving into the workforce with minimal qualifications is often associated with low socio-economic status and low educational achievement over the life course. Yet the people whose lives have been examined in this chapter did return to education and in many cases did very well. This achievement can be measured in terms of occupational status, qualifications gained and also personal satisfaction. Are these personal outcomes especially important for people whose educational start in life was unfavourable? What did the interviewees feel they gained from their university studies? In summary, the main outcomes were increased confidence, self-esteem and improved intellectual/academic capability.

The clearest outcome, mentioned by three-quarters of the women, but only one man, was increased self-confidence. The men were less likely to use the word 'confidence' but still talked about relating to people better. The following comments were typical –

> I feel much more confident now talking to people in my field. The course gave me a lot of confidence. I am more informed. (Rachel)

> I got heaps out of the course – confidence, getting up to date, losing my shyness and gaining direction. (Moira)

> Now I have more knowledge of myself and am more confident with people. I don't feel dumb any more. I can now say I don't know and ask for explanations. It's feeling good about yourself, making the best of what you have. (Eileen)

Increased self-esteem was another clear outcome of study, expressed in a variety of way, but all based on how the interviewees saw themselves. Several women talked about self-empowerment and self-knowledge, gaining a sense of satisfaction and achievement. Elsbeth said she now feels saner, happier, more contented and independent –

> Before, I sought financial and emotional support – now I can do without it. Education is the most valuable thing anyone can have. If you want to do it, go and do it – life ain't a rehearsal.

Education was valued, especially by the women early school leavers, as giving them 'something for themselves' after a period of homemaking and child rearing. For most, the experience was not only enjoyable and stimulating, but also liberating and affirming. Several people were proud of the fact that their views are now heard and respected. This came as a surprise to those who had been overlooked or ignored because of their low level of education. Barbara, aged 44 and widowed for more than ten years, left New Zealand for the first time recently and travelled alone to Britain. She feels that study had something to do with that.

Sara, aged 55, also placed a high value on education –

> When it [education] comes to you at this stage of your life it is much more precious and you value it more highly. Women at my age can feel beached and unwanted. Now I am confident and have so much more that I want to do.

Feelings of achievement were not confined to women, but there were clear elements of gender expectations in the way people analysed the outcomes of their study experience. There was an element of proving themselves, to themselves and to others, despite their early lack of educational achievement – losing shyness, making friends and being able to talk to others more confidently and articulately.

> I proved I could do it. Before I felt inferior because I didn't have an education. (Betty)

In some cases interviewees wanted to set an example for their children or wanted their children to be proud of them. References to the lives of their children and comparisons with their own experiences were common.

> I had to do a lot of catching up because of leaving school early. I would like to get an A to be like my daughter. [Without education] I wouldn't have been any more than a part-time check-out operator – that isn't me. (Moira)

> It was a reassurance that not only my children could do well at university. (Stan)

> I wanted to be like my wife and family and have interesting conversations with people. (Richard)

Support from her daughter gave Barbara confidence in her own studies and she now feels very close to her. Geraldine was acutely aware of how her example might colour her son's impressions of women. She wanted to show them that she was 'not the little woman'. Other women made comments about their husbands and wider families. Elsbeth had felt inferior alongside the academic achievements of her children and in-laws and had always been worried about failure and ridicule.

> It was important for me to get a degree to show my ex-husband I could do it, because he always thought I was dumb. I want to do honours because he hasn't got it.

Several women expressed a desire to prove something to their parents, harking back to the circumstances of their family of origin. Deborah, Sara and Indra wanted to show their mothers that they were wrong in thinking their daughters were not capable of university study and Della wanted to say to her father – 'Dad, look, I can do it!'

Male early school leavers were more likely to mention benefits in relation to people beyond their own families – in society generally and at work. Peter felt he now spoke the language of the lawyers he associated with in his work and Rex said that people could not 'pull the wool over his eyes' now. Len valued 'society's recognition of my achievement' and Sam acknowledged –

> I would not be in my job [as a social worker] without my diploma. It helped me to listen to and respect other people's opinions. It got me back to the work ethic [after being a parent at home with his children].

Among the benefits of education, all the male interviewees and two-thirds of the women mentioned improved thinking, expressive and reasoning capacities, enhanced learning skills and better focus.

> I always felt I could learn things at the highest level. I always felt clever but other people didn't realise it. I always had respect for academic cleverness – now I have it certified. I have a piece of paper which says I am clever. I feel validated. I know I am as clever as anyone and I have proved that I can stick at something. (Celia)

> I can converse on a higher level and contribute outside the family world. I am more interested in everything around me and see everything differently now. What was I doing for 20 years? I have exceeded my expectations and enriched my life. (Sara)

I have a better understanding of people. It's learning at another deeper level – I could keep going on for ever. (Rex)

There were, however, some less positive outcomes of recent university education. Three postgraduate students had experienced isolation and lack of academic support, but such problems are not solely the experience of older students. Geraldine and Celia felt their backgrounds were not quite accepted in the academic environment, with overtones of sexism and ageism. Rex and Celia both bewailed their financial situation, compared to people of their age group and Rex felt that he had not chosen his courses well.

No changes except that I am four years older – penniless and no prospects. I thought that the BA was going to be a magic ticket.

Others were apprehensive about job openings at their age. Richard thought it unlikely he could start a new career at 57 and Peter found it hard to compete with 'smart kids coming up with double degrees'.

Prospects

The postal survey asked respondents what effect they felt their study would have on aspects of their lives in the future. In total, over 80%, both men and women, thought it would have a positive or very positive effect on their work and the same was true for the early school leavers group. In other aspects of life the early leavers tended to be more positive than respondents as a whole, especially the women. Table 2.4 shows the results for future income and study prospects.

Table 2.4: Influence of education on aspects of lives in the future – percentage who considered that their study would have a positive or very positive effect.

	Early school leavers %		Total respondents %	
	Male	Female	Male	Female
Future Income	76	79	62	64
Future Study	73	76	67	71

The majority of the interviewees also saw their experience of university study as positive and affirming for their future lives. Some looked forward only to completing their current qualification, but several had plans for further study. Alan wanted to go on to a doctorate although 'my wife says it's her turn and she has been patient'. Ruth had a study schedule to take her to a PhD at age 70.

Many had developed new careers. Sam had secured a social work job and wanted to earn some money before possibly returning to do a Master's and Len had work in architecture related to the conservation of heritage buildings. Barbara was working towards being a childcare centre supervisor. Sometimes the career was not directly connected to their new qualifications. Carla now wanted to go into website design – 'it is no crazier than me doing a degree'. Elsbeth was writing a book of short stories and had an interest in counselling. Eileen was looking for work in political analysis and Moira (who says she has 'not even blossomed yet!') wanted to move into communications and the media.

The people in or near retirement were less oriented towards careers, but still viewed education as a positive contribution to their future. Several talked about keeping their minds active as they aged, continuing to develop and to contribute. Deirdre said – 'I feel sorry for widows who do nothing.' They were able to enjoy education for itself after many years of putting either career or family first.

> After many years of being a wife, mother and working to assist my children through university it was now time to do my own thing. (Elsbeth)

Conclusion

The experiences presented in this chapter show how education at university level (although this could apply at other levels) has been the means for people who left school early not only to gain qualifications and improve their career prospects, but also to improve their confidence and self-esteem and affirm their worth. In other words, their identities as individuals have been strengthened. They have been able to prove to partners, families and the wider world that they are capable of academic achievement, in the course of this setting an example for or taking a lead from their own children as they develop into adults.

In a more practical way, examples have been presented to show how access to university study has opened doors for further study as well as career development and new career opportunities, many of them ambitious and imaginative. The advantages gained by early school leavers through their educational achievements have allowed them to transcend the barriers of class and gender expectations which may have limited their early educational development, giving them capacities, confidence and personal resources which will stand them in good stead for the rest of their lives.

Notes

1   Official Yearbook figures.

2   School Certificate is a national examination system in which candidates may sit up to six subjects and are now credited with a grade for each subject. However, School Certificate does not qualify a student to proceed straight away to university. University Entrance examinations have always taken place in the sixth form, generally at age 17 to 18.

3   In New Zealand, entry to university at stage 1 undergraduate level in most cases does not require any prior qualifications from age 21 onwards.

4   The choices of motivation type were –
    • work related – to acquire new knowledge/qualifications for improving job performance or prospects
    • personal development and fulfilment – to acquire knowledge for its own sale and to develop oneself more fully
    • to set an example for my children or grandchildren.

3

VICTORIOUS MEN – MEN STUDYING FULL-TIME

Jane Renwick

Invisible men

While there is a considerable amount of research on older women 'returning' to education, there are few studies that focus on men. The issues relating to women juggling the commitments of study with the responsibilities of caring for their families are well documented (and explored in the New Zealand context in several other chapters), but little attention is given to the experiences of men who move from the role of full-time worker (and possibly family breadwinner) to that of full-time student. This chapter explores the experiences of 13 men aged 40–59 who were full-time students at Victoria University. The 13 were drawn from the total of 84 men among the postal survey respondents who came into the full-time category.[1] In fact, men are over-represented among full-time students aged 40-plus – forming 37% of full-timers, 27% of part-timers and 29% of the older students group as a whole.

Because of the lack of existing literature this was an exploratory exercise, using a life course framework, in common with other studies reported in this book. The interview questions were qualitative, exploring the men's experiences in the lead up to university study and how university fitted into their lives. Because the group was small it is not realistic to link the experiences of these 13 men to a larger population – for example all men over forty studying full-time at Victoria, or any other university. Hence the material is analysed in qualitative and thematic terms. Nevertheless, some inferences can be made and some illustrative stories presented to throw light on the experiences of a group of adult learners who differ from the stereotype presented in chapter one, by their gender and by the fact that they are studying full-time.

Schooling and the next steps

The 13 men had a mixture of memories surrounding their primary school years. Two of them said that this was the most productive and enjoyable period in their early education. But six had less positive memories, arising from difficulties with school authority or from unhappy circumstances in their home life. One man's father had died just prior to his birth and his mother had five young children to bring up. Another lived in a family where there was an unstable relationship between his parents. For four men their memories of primary school were coloured by the adjustments they had to make each time their families had moved house. One man went to a total of seven schools, another to eight. In hindsight the former said –

> It didn't help with the socialisation of us at school. We went to different schools in different towns. It was a given that we kids would cope. In subsequent adult conversations with my parents they never expressed any regret, it was a given that that was what we did as a family.

In general the men reported having more difficulties during their secondary school years in comparison to primary schooling. These difficulties included a general dislike of school, absence due to a long illness, truancy and other problems with discipline. Peer pressure was sometimes a factor –

> School was not so good, I didn't achieve well, there was too much going on in my life. I left school at age 18 with Sixth Form Certificate in three subjects. I would have left in the fifth form if it hadn't been for the rugby.

> I was in with a class of lower socio-economic kids who did not want to learn. They were there under protest. It wasn't an environment conducive to learning. I have never been athletic – but all these guys were. I was the smallest and easily intimidated. When I was 15, I sat School Certificate and failed. I didn't want to leave without qualifications so I went back. I opted to go into a B class instead of an upper fifth. These kids wanted to learn and it made all the difference.

Some difficulties were related to aspects of their home lives, such as further moves, the loss of a father and family illness, abusive family environments, marital breakdown, drug and alcohol problems.

My father died when I was 12–13. I did School Certificate and then left school at 15 to work and support my mum.

I really enjoyed school [but] my marks in the sixth form dropped, I was bored. I left at 16, my parents were splitting up. I wanted to be adult grown-up about it, I got a radio servicing apprenticeship.

I left school at 17 having failed UE, I wasn't accredited. I sat and missed by seven marks. That's been a regret of mine. Dad shifted again, and Mum and Dad said if I wanted to sit UE again I had to do it in the new town we were going to, at a new high school. I didn't want to do that. Dad got me a job in the civil service . . .

Parental expectations also played a part – as seen in the previous chapter for early school leavers.

My experience of school was indifferent. I left with School Certificate, which was regarded as adequate in those days. There was no emphasis in my family on academic achievement, there were no books in the house or any reading.

Thus the majority of the men left school without University Entrance and, considering the various reasons given for leaving school, it is of no surprise that none went straight to university. Most of them lacked the necessary qualifications and further study was not a general expectation in their families. Indeed, the majority of young people at the time were leaving school with no educational qualifications (cf early school leavers in chapter two). Looking back, one man compared his situation with that of his nephew –

A nephew of mine went to university. We were close. I think I would have had a role model influence there. I have another nephew who went but we weren't that close. I think university for him is an expectation of his generation.

Looking for work was a natural next step for the men once they left school. Work was readily available and job hunting was an easy task. One man said –

In those days you could just read a paper in the morning and have a job at the end of the day. The labour market was really active in the early 1970s.

In their first year out of school seven of the men took on semi-skilled factory, service or labouring work, two men began apprenticeships, two worked in the public service, and two had white collar jobs in the private sector.

Two men did pursue a university career within a few years of leaving school. One was encouraged by his family and he was the only one who mentioned that going to university was amongst his plans after he left school.

> I had trouble with authority and left school after the sixth form. I think I was probably expelled . . . I went to Massey University for one term. I had missed out on the seventh form but I had always intended to go to university . . . I couldn't cut it, I gave up pretty quickly . . . I then moved to Wellington in 1978. I enrolled at Victoria in 1979, I had always intended to finish. It was unfinished business.

The second man went to university as a young adult because he was encouraged by his boss –

> I then became an assistant to a research chemist. He convinced me to go to university. I went from 1961 to 1964 . . . and I ended up in 1964 with a BSc Honours in chemistry.

Another man mentioned that his parents had always presented university as their preferred option for his future. But it was over thirty years on before he completed his first degree. This man is one of only two in the group whose parents had a tertiary education.

Adult life – favourable and adverse circumstances

Between secondary school and the time when they became students at Victoria University, the men had a variety of life experiences, some favourable and some adverse. Indeed, for four of the men trauma would be a more accurate word than adversity.

Favourable circumstances
Eight men, including the two oldest, described their lives as young adults in largely favourable terms, linking this mainly to their work and career histories. Stability in employment was seen as a positive factor by four men who had enjoyed continuous employment and the

certainty of permanent jobs. Opportunities for training were another beneficial aspect of work life. Five men had acquired training related to their occupation, in police work, welding, and management/accountancy.

Other sources of satisfaction were flexible careers, work which they enjoyed and wanted to do, and promotion. One man had a career that advanced to a top position in his profession. As a consequence, when he was later made redundant he received a considerable sum of money as a severance payment. Now in his mid-50s, he sees himself in a privileged position because of his work history and because he knows his skills are still highly valued if he chooses to take on work again. Another man who rose through the ranks described a favourable period in his life where he enjoyed the 'perks' of seniority and the generosity of his employer.

> I got promoted again and moved to a larger branch and got friendly with head office. The company got merged with (another) and they cut back on all extras. Things got tight. I got dissatisfied and I wanted to step down to another position. I got the position and I got less money.

Adversity

On the other hand, seven men also spoke of unpleasant times in their lives, and shared aspects of that adversity that were very personal. In several cases this was related to involvement with drugs and crime.[2] One man had been present during the accidental, but most likely suicidal, death of a close friend. Later he married this man's girlfriend and now, many years later, has the enormous task of caring for his wife who is a long-term, multidependent drug user.

> Difficult, it is really difficult. In some ways it is fine but in some ways it is not. (She) is okay when she is zonked and she splits her medication . . . When she is stressed and anxious she is demanding of my time and attention. She is often touchy and angry and there is abuse.

Another man who had been a multidependent drug user himself spoke of the difficulties associated with this lifestyle. He eventually came to Victoria after several years of making inquiries about university courses and during this time he overcame an addiction to Valium so he could commit himself to the work required for his degree.

In two of the five cases involving drugs/crime, the men had been to prison. For both men prison had been a traumatic experience, involving violence and illness. One man began his tertiary study – a polytechnic course – whilst he was in prison.[3] Since leaving prison, both men had spent several years doing tertiary studies including polytechnic courses and extramural university studies.

Nine of the 13 men interviewed had children and in only two cases were all their children living independently. In three cases, family adversity involved tragedies associated with their children. These men had all experienced the loss of a child sometime over the last eight years. Two children had died after long periods of illness or serious disability and one had died as the result of an accident. The children had ranged in age from teenager to young adults at the time of their deaths.

The impact of these deaths was different for each man. One man gave little detail as his son had been living away from his family for some time. The second took a philosophical viewpoint, perhaps because daughter's life-threatening condition had been known about from a very early age. The third man had lost his child at the age of 17, following the sudden discovery of an illness which had lasted for six years. He told a graphic and emotional story of the impact this had had on him. He also suggested that his later determination to do well at university could be attributed in part to these emotions.

> I fought for marks; I would fight for half a mark. I argued all the time, I had more control over the future but with my son I didn't have any control. I was obsessive.

Two men had entered into a more recent period of adversity, occurring during their time at university. The cases are similar in some aspects – the wives of both men had breakdowns during this time and both had been separated from their families.

The first man came to university after he had been made redundant. His wife and preschool children had been dependent on him for income and he had trouble finding further work. Despite his wife's opposition he became a full-time student. After a suicide in her family his wife suffered a breakdown, was hospitalised and later the children were removed from the family home. This man kept up his full-time study, and the family was back together in 2001. Recently he had been subject to more pressure as his extended family also wanted him to give up his study.

While the second man was at university he 'came out' about his childhood experience of sexual abuse by his stepfather.

> My abuse did interrupt my life. I was 38 when I got some help, and I told my wife about it at the same time . . . After counselling things started to happen and I focused on study.

At the same time he was coping with full-time study and part-time work. The pressure was great on himself and his wife.

> I spoke to my wife and said I had to study, we knew it would be tough. It probably cost me my marriage. I switched off and concentrated on university. My wife took on all the responsibility, all the worry and other things. I didn't participate in family life. I was determined and focused, the stress got really bad and I almost threw it in. The things going on at home were very stressful . . . She got quite sick.

Several of the men who faced family adversity took on extra and onerous activities, possibly more than they need have done, given their circumstances. One did two degrees simultaneously whilst working part-time, and the other took on mountain biking several times a week. What was the relationship between the 'go hard' attitude of these men and the trauma/adversity which they were facing?

A wide range of coping strategies has been put forward to help individuals to cope with adversity. Six such strategies, suggested in a recent New Zealand book, reflect some of the reactions mentioned by the interviewees –

- gaining confidence through developing abilities
- keeping busy and putting energy into hard work
- a commitment to carry on
- getting on with the job at hand despite the problems
- fulfilling self-potential
- having goals and a vision for the future to work towards[4]

Combining work, family and study

This discussion raises a comment from my own point of view, as a woman who has been a university student (Jane Renwick). It interests me, in light of my experiences of caring for my young family, that several of the men I interviewed had the capacity to take on so much activity, including full-time study, as a coping strategy in the face of their adversity. Two of the men made it clear that this was because their wives did everything for their families. I doubt whether a sample of women studying full-time with similar experiences would be in the position to focus so intently on their own activities, to withdraw from the burdens of family and thus to distract themselves from their misfortunes. It appears that, in both instances, it was simply assumed that their wives would take over the family maintenance, without any prior negotiation.

However, there were other men who did not adopt this assumption of male advantage. One man had provided care for various family members over a numbers of years and at times withdrew from university to do this. The other had to assume the caregiver role when adversity struck. It had been difficult for him too and his university work had been compromised as a result.

> My family commitments are quite extreme. It has been more difficult since the children came back at the beginning of the year. Last year was difficult for different reasons. My partner hates me studying, I failed two papers last year.

Combining work, family and study responsibilities is a challenge for all older students and is a recurrent theme throughout this book. However, most of the men interviewed did not report having difficulties with the combination. The exceptions were the two men who were involved with primary caregiving for their families and one other who had to travel for two hours to university and had taken on a short-term work contract to boost his household income.

The remaining ten reported no real difficulties apart from the need manage their time so they could pursue recreation or be with friends or family. The single men had few problems because they only had to care for themselves. Even men with young families reported having no real difficulties because they could rely on their wives. One man said –

It was easy enough – I had come from doing more than 40 hours (work per week). It was just the same commitment. The only thing was that I had a timeline, and I could only be unemployed for two and a half years.

It is interesting to compare the situation of this group of men with the 'juggling' which mature women at university have frequently to manage. These experiences feature predominantly in the research literature on female students and are illustrated in other chapters of this book. Feminist writing has a long tradition of addressing the issue of unequal roles and responsibilities between men and women. This body of work contains many findings on the undervaluing of women's work and the conflict inherent in the roles women are expected to perform.[5]

In summing up his own position, one of the men acknowledged the gender inequality inherent in his domestic relationship. When asked how he managed combining work, family and other activities, he said –

Fine, no problem I had a supportive partner. I had space at home, it was close to varsity. I had white middle class male privilege. I did take up more housework but it had to be suggested to me.

Motives for full-time university study

Much of the literature about adult education concentrates on class as an important characteristic.[6] A few men identified themselves as having a 'working class background' or being 'middle class', but the small size of the interview group does not allow issues of class to be pursued in any depth. Pākehā New Zealand is frequently portrayed as an egalitarian society.[7] This was borne out in the experience of the interviewees, whose life courses illustrated a fairly fluid state of social mobility. Several men moved relatively easily from humble beginnings to better circumstances later in life and others migrated socially in the reverse direction. Here are two examples –

My father was a wharfie. He just emigrated . . . Mum emigrated by herself. She immigrated as a sole person to the 'lucky country'.

I had gone from a childhood of middle class, to being with the dregs of the city. I was used to being in the company of criminals, pimps and prostitutes. I didn't want to go back to this environment. I disassociated myself with those people and hung out with an old sports crowd.

The decision to come to university was not overtly linked with social or class mobility in the minds of the men who were interviewed, nor did they talk about attaining a social position they had previously been denied. Instead, the decision to study at university level was related much more clearly to paid work factors. The men believed that going to university would improve their position as older men in the workforce.

Career options
Eleven out of the 13 men had come to university believing that as older men they would have better work options with a university qualification.[8] Sometimes their choice of degree was based on long-term interests –

> The guidance counsellor said why drive trucks, why not study and get a job via university. At first I was sceptical but it is where I started off . . . I wasn't thinking about money I was thinking of interest. I was advised to do a degree where I liked what I was doing so it would help me achieve the qualification. This is the best way for me.

> I know I won't get rich, I only continue for the love of it. I'm a bit scared about going out to the workplace and competing with young people.

The publicity material used to encourage participation at university often suggests that apprehensive mature students build on existing interests. This recognises that older students have high expectations of themselves in relation to their work and the marks they will receive.[9]

However, the majority of interviewees did not necessarily have much prior interest in the subject material they would study. They were focused on achieving a degree which would give them a pass to an interesting occupation.

> I'm going to fit as many meaty career-orientated papers in as I can to improve my job prospects. Because of my age my career prospects aren't great so I have to catch their eye somehow. I can improve my chances like a hand of cards, with the right core papers that relate to my major.

It was not my first choice of study, English and writing would have been. But I did a (subject) degree because it is more commercially viable to get a job with.

The degree I've got isn't the degree I planned on getting (which is) of little worth in the job market. This is the reason I decided to do the MA, because the degree wasn't going to get me a job.

The four men studying law all chose their degrees in the belief that they would be tickets to better employment prospects. All had previous histories of job promotions and, at times, interesting careers. All had worked in occupations which involved interaction with lawyers in some capacity. These men viewed training as a lawyer as a favourable way to exit their previous career, transfer some of their expertise and pursue another occupation. One man said –

I did the law degree to get out of Human Resources.

He also said –

I thought I could do it, I had worked a lot with lawyers. I thought it was something I could succeed at. I thought I would have no trouble getting work, although that is not right.

Part of the motivation to study law had been diminishing opportunities for satisfaction and promotion in their previous occupations, frequently associated with restructuring and downsizing in the workplace environments of the 1990s.

There were no promotional opportunities due to there being too many seniors in the (area of work) job market.

Another said –

I was looking at leaving the (organisation), I didn't like the direction the sector was going in.

Inherent in the attitudes of men who saw university study as a career-orientated move was the perception that older age meant diminishing work opportunities. Although this was based on their own experiences, this perception is not unfounded. In New Zealand the Equal Opportunities Section of the State Services Commission published a booklet on the subject of age discrimination to inform the debate on amending the Human Rights Act in 1991. This reviewed the research here and overseas and concluded that from the age of 40 workers were likely to be subject to age discrimination.[10] A later Massey University survey of nearly one thousand mature unemployed workers in New Zealand showed that the age at which discrimination occurs for mature workers is falling, both here and internationally.[11]

How well the men in this research manage with their qualifications, in the face of such discrimination, remains to be seen. Similar difficulties are illustrated in chapter eight, which looks at people who had been made redundant. Since graduating, four men found difficulty in finding the jobs they wanted and others had work which they saw only as interim, while waiting for better opportunities. One man was still unemployed and concerned about his future. He said –

> Six months ago I would have said yes it was all worthwhile. But trying to find work is not easy. The degree has not made me really employable.

Studying for interest
Two men out of the 13 came to university as full-time students, not in the hope that study would lead to employment options, but to pursue degrees purely on the basis of interest. These differed in two other ways from the 11 men discussed before. Firstly, they were older, aged 55 and 59, whereas the others were in the range from 41 to 50. Secondly, both had been made redundant from senior positions in the workforce. As a consequence, both had savings to fall back on and they had also received generous severance payments. Their financial circumstances had thus given these men a period of financial security, in which studying full-time for interest was a viable option. One man, who had done a career-orientated degree much earlier in life, said –

> For me I wanted to maximise my potential as a person. After 40 years I was a bit apprehensive. I was testing the water, I had every intention of finishing my degree. . . . I wanted to have other cultural insights. I had led a fairly sheltered life as a child.

Unlike the younger men, these two were not set on working full-time again. They were looking towards retirement, probably a little earlier than the expected age of around 65. This is despite the fact that both men were studying at postgraduate level in subjects (management, economics, science, and technology) related to areas in which New Zealand has a shortage of skills.

The experience of studying at Victoria

The interviewees were unanimous that studying at Victoria University had brought them enjoyable learning experiences and intellectual nourishment.

> It was a stimulating environment – a different atmosphere than working in an office.

> I love learning new things. I sit in class fascinated even if others find it boring.

Second among their 'likes' were the social aspects of university study. This related to group work and tutorials and also in the wider setting of friendships formed with other students and academic staff, whilst the men were at university.

Their dislikes were more diverse. Only one man could not think of anything he disliked. Eight people commented unfavourably on the administration and standards of teaching at Victoria. These criticisms were from a range of faculties. Here are quotes from five of the men –

> I wanted to do honours. Of all the courses I wanted to do three of the four were not available. So my subjects are my second and third choices, the first choice courses were cancelled on me. This really annoys me about the university.

> The theoretical approach and the arrogance of some lecturers, their general aloofness, some were brilliant but some were not.

> There is a major difference between career professionals and those who do it ad hoc. For example, in my advanced [subject] class I had six tutors. It shows the difference between lecturers who are committed and those who are not. I wanted more continuity.

> You learn in spite of the useless lecturers. Some attitudes of lecturers were inappropriate but standing in front of a room full of youngsters they could get away with it.

There is an inconsistency in the marking, it is really an inaccurate assessment scale. . . . It is rigid and they hid behind the rules, so you've got to get around the rules, it takes time and determination. This doesn't guarantee success.

The second most common problem area was the cost involved in full-time study. One man in particular punctuated his interview with references to what a burden this had been for him. He had been to university as a young adult when students had an allowance, holiday employment programmes and no tuition fees. At one stage he said –

In actual fact my (marital) separation made me financially better off because I qualified for a student allowance because I was poor.

Concerns about the costs of study were compounded by uncertainties about future employment and whether their investment would be recouped at a later date.

The insecurity of not knowing whether this will lead to work for me. I've committed myself to a student loan so I have to have a plan. I feel I'm getting old, it makes it harder to get work.

Conclusion

The title for this research came to mind because analysis of the interviews suggested that the men were indeed triumphant in their achievements as students. None of them had progressed all the way through secondary school and many had experienced considerable adversity in their later lives. For some the adversity coincided with their time spent as university students. Hence the concept of 'victorious men', because they embodied a sense of great accomplishment despite the setbacks which still hindered them. However, as noted, these achievements were frequently made possible through the support of a female partner, who took on the necessary family and caring work.

All 13 men recognised that their studies had benefited them in terms of personal growth. But this positive outcome must be balanced against their aspirations for rewarding and interesting jobs. Whether the men will achieve this objective is as yet unknown, but some of the men's comments suggest that the outlook is not wholly positive, given age discrimination and a tight job market. This aligns with the conclusions in chapter eight, on the redundancy group.

Another consideration is the investment in time and money which the men made to pursue their studies and the opportunity cost of earnings forgone during their time as full-time students. For one man the cost of a failed marriage might be added too and family hardship may well have been an additional cost to wives and children. Taking all this into consideration it is of concern that more than half of the interviewees were critical of aspects of their education. These criticisms are significant, coming from mature people with experience of the world and need to be taken seriously (along with other findings from the Victoria University study) by institutions of tertiary education.

Despite these concerns, the men took pride in their learning and in their academic achievements. Their stories epitomise an important aspect of New Zealand's egalitarian education system. For 60 or more years people aged 20 years and over have had the right of provisional admission to a New Zealand University, and have been given the opportunity to prove their ability to meet university standards. However, a recent report of the Tertiary Education Advisory Committee has recommended that students should not be allowed into university unless and until they achieve University Entrance qualifications.[12] If this suggested change in policy had been operating when the men decided to go to university, eight would have been denied entry and hence a 'second chance' at higher education.

Notes

1 Many of the men studying full-time at Victoria University did not make themselves available for the interview stage, so the interview group was supplemented by one man who met the prescription, but who was not a survey respondent. The group of 13 cannot be considered a representative sample.

2 The terms 'drugs and crime' are included together to protect the identities of the men in this group. During interviewing some men discussed their own experiences in these areas, but for the purposes of this research, it is not necessary to provide further details of individual cases.

3 Polytechnic courses have been traditionally recommended as particularly appropriate for prison education. (Prison Review Committee, 1989).

4 Paterson (1997) pp.180–6.

5 Redding (1992), Tong (1989).

6 Sargant (1997).

7   Dunstall (1981).

8   One of these men said he later changed his view about his education being primarily for employment purposes. After doing two degrees he developed an interest in a specific topic, and his aim was to continue in this area through further degrees. Now he cares less about the 'employment' prospects associated with his qualifications. Instead it is more important to him, at this point, to have an interest in the subjects he has taken to a postgraduate level.

9   Bonnie Dewart 15/10/1997.

10 Some research findings suggested that for certain groups of women the prevalence of age discrimination occurred from the earlier age of 35 (Rendell (1992)).

11 Henderson 22/12/2001, McGregor (2001).

12 Tertiary Education Advisory Commission (2001).

4

OLDER MĀORI AS STUDENTS –
'I'M FINALLY MOVING FROM BEING A SPECTATOR
TO BEING A PARTICIPANT IN MY OWN CULTURE'

Maamari Stephens and Te Ripowai Higgins

Māori and university

It quickly becomes obvious, when faced with a roomful of Māori students of any age that tertiary education is sometimes viewed as a type of key to a magic kingdom of employment, better incomes and escape from real or threatened poverty and the awful inevitability of bottom-of-the-heap statistics. There is a sense, in such a gathering, of a turning back of the tide, as Māori people reclaim control over their destinies and their socio-political rap sheets. Such students recognise the odds they have beaten merely to be present in the room. However, the struggle to overcome odds and achieve participation in tertiary education is not restricted to Māori students. What *is* unique for many Māori tertiary students is their search for cultural redemption and reintegration within such institutions. The schools of higher learning in New Zealand were created as the purveyors of western academic disciplines; yet they have also become, in the last thirty years or so, bastions of Māori cultural heritage.

For mature Māori students tertiary education can be a painful reminder that they have been unable to absorb traditional knowledge of reo and tikanga from their own whānau, hapū and marae. Many such students, having necessarily lost much of their heritage as a direct or indirect result of primary and secondary education, recognise the irony in entering tertiary education to try and recover something of what has been lost. This chapter will explore some of the experiences and conflicts faced by mature Māori students in tertiary education at Victoria University in Wellington.

The bigger picture

Among the 959 respondents to the 'Education in Mid and Later Life' postal questionnaire were 75 students of Māori descent, aged 40 and over. Information on this group is referred to in this chapter, but the material presented is largely qualitative, based on the results of a focus group that was held in December 2001. The circumstances of the focus group members did not necessarily align with the data for the Māori group as a whole.[1] The focus group, as will be discussed shortly, offered the opportunity for a few selected mature Māori students to talk in more in depth about their experiences at Victoria University.

Some context

According to the 'Closing the Gaps' report released by Te Puni Kōkiri in May 2000, more Māori than ever before are completing degree programmes.[2] The percentage of Māori student enrolments as a proportion of all tertiary enrolments reached 16.1% in 2000, up from 14.3% percent in 1997. It is significant for this study, however, that while Māori rates of participation in tertiary education are less than half those for non-Māori for 18–21 year olds, the rates for the 35-plus age group are higher for Māori. (See Table 4.1.)

This information suggests that the experience of older Māori students may be different to their non-Māori counterparts. As will be seen in this chapter the mature Māori students spoken to are subject to some cultural imperatives that mark them out a little differently, not only from their non-Māori counterparts but also from younger Māori tertiary students.

Introducing the mature Māori students

We spoke to eight mature Māori students at various stages of their tertiary careers. They hail from various iwi around the North Island including Ngāti Toa Rangatira, Ngāti Porou, Ngāti Ranginui, Te Ati Awa, and Tuhoe. Four males and four females, they had been studying a variety of subjects, including law, education, theatre and film, Māori and Māori studies. Three of the participants were first-year students: Tere (female, 53), Miriam (47) and Simon (50). Two of the students had already completed one Bachelor's degree: Irihapeti (45) and Mahara (male 59).[3] One student had completed a Diploma in Māori Studies and was continuing with his degree papers (Jack 61). One student

Table 4.1: Māori and non-Māori age-specific tertiary participation rates, 1998

Age group	Māori (%)	non-Māori (%)	Disparity gap (% points)
<16	2.1	2.1	0.0
17	6.2	8.8	2.6
18	17.3	36.4	19.1
19	17.9	42.3	24.4
20	18.5	40.9	22.4
21	15.9	34.1	18.2
22	13.6	24.6	11.0
23	11.4	17.8	6.5
24	9.8	13.9	4.2
25–29	7.8	9.7	1.9
30–34	6.9	7.4	0.5
35–39	6.8	6.3	-0.5
40+	3.4	2.1	-1.3

Data sources: Ministry of Education, unpublished tables, 1999; Statistics New Zealand, population estimates, 1999.
Notes: (1) These rates are calculated using Statistics New Zealand population estimates as at 30 June 1998. (2) The 'disparity gap' figure is the percentage point difference between Māori and non-Māori. The closer to 0 the disparity, the more similar the outcomes for Māori and non-Māori.

(Mitchell 30) had just completed a postgraduate qualification, his BA (hons). Two students were completing conjoint qualifications – Mereraina (female 35) and Mitchell. All of these students had studied or were studying Māori language and/or Māori tikanga. All group members are parents; five of the eight are grandparents. The group ranged in age from 30 to 61 with six of the eight over 45.

Reasons for coming to university

The results of the postal survey showed that the most important trigger for Māori students (particularly for female students) to attend tertiary study later in life was a reduction in the demand for childcare. Job loss was the next most important factor. However, the focus group members did not strongly identify these factors in their discussions.

Pressure from others
Jack, Irihapeti, Miriam and Mereraina described family and external pressures to attend university. Jack humorously described being 'forced' to attend university by his Victoria University-educated daughter, while Irihapeti found herself being encouraged to enrol at university by older adults that she respected, with some standing in the Māori community. Miriam felt herself being drawn to Victoria in particular to build up her links with her own iwi and by acknowledging that Victoria was the closest university to her own Ngāti Toa Rangatira maunga and marae. Mereraina, in her decision to study law, was influenced by the opinions of Māori lawyers who had passed through Victoria University's law faculty. For all students, regardless of outside pressures, the decision was ultimately personal, particularly the decision to learn the Māori language and concluding that university would be the best place to achieve that goal.

Careers and credentialism
The younger members of the group (Irihapeti, Mitchell and Mereraina) had more career-orientated goals for their tertiary study than did the older members. Mitchell and Irihapeti reported that the relative scarcity of Māori students at university could work in favour of such students in respect to job opportunities in certain fields such as psychology and the sciences. As stated by Mitchell –

> the networks and the people I met did not give me extra mana, but doors opened.

There was little indication among the older group members that their participation at university was triggered by a need for qualifications. For the three first-year students the actual qualification seemed to be of less concern than day-to-day survival of the university workload. All the first-year students were still concentrating on finishing the requirements for their Diplomas in Māori Studies (Tohu Māoritanga) before committing themselves to completing degree programmes.

Transmission of knowledge
All focus group members spoke of their learning specifically as a legacy to be passed on to future generations. The postal survey also identified 'setting an example for children or grandchildren' as an important

motivation for 44% of the mature Māori students. Focus group members tended to speak of a 'duty' or an 'obligation' to pass on what they have already learned and were yet to learn at university; not only to their own whānau, but to other Māori in their communities. Mitchell saw his obligation in terms of utu, or reciprocity leading him in his own right to become a teacher of the things he had learned.

A huge motivation is the people who have passed away –

> it is the principle of reciprocity. What are you saying about your teacher if you refused to use te reo? You have to pay these people back. You must promote te reo somehow. That's what it's about.

Experiencing university

Once the mature Māori students reach university only a small part of the battle has been won. The practical day-to-day realities of attending lectures and passing assignments are hard enough. Two-thirds of Māori respondents in the postal survey indicated that they faced difficulties in returning to study – especially time demands posed by work and family. The focus group noted the added weight of undertaking a personal journey to mend old wounds that have resulted from cultural dislocation. Sometimes those wounds are healed. Sometimes new wounds occur.

Practical obstacles

While practical barriers to tertiary education, such as student loans and other financial matters, were mentioned by the group participants, most of the perceived obstacles to achieving tertiary education centred on childcare and other issues to do with whānau responsibilities. As stated by Simon and Mereraina it seemed, as mature students, that their family responsibilities were heavier than for younger Māori students.

> I'm more or less the carer in the whānau and it doesn't matter if I'm in a lecture I have to set time aside – distressing sometimes but I can't run away from my responsibilities

> One of the biggest problems is the lack of quality time with family – time is lost. It's choice but it hurts – it's really hard when you choose lecturers over your children – you see their disappointment.

Jack acknowledged that male and female mature students make such sacrifices.

No matter what, we make the sacrifices to be here. But some don't and then for them it is too late.

Age was acknowledged as an obstacle by some of the students. Miriam and Mahara saw their age as an impediment to absorbing new information.

Age catches up and it is a handicap.

Kids minds are like sponges but with mature students, it's much harder.

Mereraina saw her maturity as an advantage. She felt she had better focus than younger Māori students, but found that much of the advice given to her by others was geared to younger people.

People say – don't get 'stressed out' – but you don't know what they mean. Tell us what you *mean*! Such kōrero might help young ones – but not mature students. But being mature is also your biggest advantage. You've already planned out why you are there. Talking to mature people helps because they have been there.

The changing perceptions of others
Once at university many of the students reported that their family and friends tended to treat and regard them differently. As stated by Mereraina –

To [attend university] moves you out of one realm into another, 'you're one of those expected to go back to the iwi'.

A common theme for the women of the group was some reluctance to be seen as somehow 'better' than other members of their families and Māori communities because of their entry into university education. Tere noted that, as the first of her family to attend university, she had since received comments such as 'I bet you think you're neat' from friends and family. These comments appeared on the one hand to be negative, but also indicated that somehow Tere had gained a greater level of status and visibility in the eyes of others; an idea which made her slightly uncomfortable. Irihapeti also felt this awkwardness, stating that she sometimes felt other Māori saw her as 'showing off . . . who does she think she is?' Miriam noted a perception that university education may not gain her any further standing in the eyes of some at her own marae: 'a BA means nothing in the Māori world'. On the other hand, Mereraina keenly felt the expectations of her family that she would excel at university because of the mana of her grandfather who was a very well known kaumatua. Sharing his last name has, in some senses, been a special burden for Mereraina to bear. This is because she fears being seen as better than her family and her peers, but also because of fears that she may let her family down during her years at Victoria University.

By comparison the male participants reported less anxiety about being perceived as separate from or different to the communities they had come from. Simon, even though he experienced whakamā in his first year at university, had experienced only positive support from his family and friends, particularly his brothers, one a minister, the other a lecturer –

> I had been taught: know who you are. The day I decided to go to university I had a lot of support and I thank them for the strength they have given me.

Four of the eight group members were the first in their families to attend university and felt this fact to be important because they were now role models for the rest of their family. Mahara is now pleasantly surprised that his experiences are influencing his own grandchildren.

> I'm most fortunate in that my grandchildren wish to follow in my footsteps. If they do . . . who knows – but they say that now and that makes me really proud.

Finding something that had been lost
Te Hoe Nuku Roa, the Department of Māori Studies at Massey University prepared a report entitled 'Māori Profiles: An Integrated Approach to Policy and Planning' in 1996. The first phase of a longitudinal study of Māori households, it found that a sense of security in cultural identity could be a determinative factor in the type of education sought by Māori at all levels.[4]

> This study shows that those whose cultural identity is *less secure* may feel more strongly about pursuing educational options which admit a kaupapa Māori approach as well as Māori based and Māori addition options. (Emphasis added.)

Arguably, this connection between security in cultural identity and participation in tertiary education is reflected by the observations of the group members. For most, going to university was a chance to replace aspects of their heritage that had been lost during their lifetime or even before they were born. Miriam, while feeling secure in her own marae and community, felt keenly the lack of her language, while she refused to see people who speak Māori as better than her. Irihapeti spoke of her desire to learn her father's language, a language that had been 'bashed' out of him before her birth. Similar to many other urban Māori, Irihapeti spoke about learning what being Māori actually meant. She felt the pressure to take her learning 'home' to her own people.

I couldn't go 'home'. Where was 'home'?

Mitchell observed that in his experience some Māori students relied on their own unique cultural identities to enable them to retain a sense of cultural integrity within the university environment. Sometimes such reliance becomes an obstacle to learning in the university environment.

One of my saddest observations is that some of the obstacles are real – others are not. I hate seeing obstacles students put in front of themselves. For example in [first-year Māori language lectures] one student wouldn't use macrons, because their kaumatua said not to. Another student was annoyed because Pākehā students were getting A's – both left. These are obstacles students put in front of themselves. There are ways to fight but be smart.

Irihapeti saw these 'obstacles' as a reflection of the disinheritance experienced by so many students who then became sensitive to perceived insult or further degradation of their own heritage and language.

That is part of the pain of growing up. Disinheritance is in my face and learning Te Reo is a constant reminder of how I lost it.

Notwithstanding the pain and difficulty that accompanies their learning as mature Māori students, Tere, Simon, Mahara, Mereraina and Irihapeti all spoke of achieving in their learning more of a sense of active belonging to their Māori heritage.

I was a spectator for many years and I never understood a word of what they said . . . but now I'm slowly becoming a participant.

The sting in the tail

The 'Education in Mid and Later Life' postal survey showed that most older Māori students did not feel inhibited by institutional barriers such as teaching and course arrangements. In a similar vein, everyone in the focus group spoke positively of their learning experience. However, they did indicate that the enjoyment of their time at university was tempered by the recognition that they needed to attend an essentially Pākehā institution in order to learn their own language and heritage. This recognition is reflected in the ambiguity felt by many of the students at having to learn Māori language through a lecture-based system. However, two were comfortable with such a structured system, as it carried on from their own positive learning experiences at secondary school. As described by Irihapeti –

> I'm used to learning in the European way. So university is good, we get the nuts and bolts. I've been able to 'get it'.

For other students the 'nuts and bolts' approach to language learning is viewed as an impediment to accessing the depth of the Māori language. For Simon, learning Māori through grammatical structures proved problematic –

> We have to learn Māori properly, but we also have to learn English too. What's an *adjective*? I get left behind by the other students in the class who know.

Irihapeti and Simon expressed their disappointment that some non-Māori are able to learn Māori more quickly than themselves.

> I came in and I thought I would know more than the Pākehā people in my class and often they whip up an A and you are struggling to get B. It's a triple whammy: I don't want to have to go to Pākehā to learn my own language and tikanga. I can do it now but it still stings.

Tere and Miriam protested against the squeezing of language learning into fast-paced fifty-minute lectures and language laboratory sessions. They saw such teaching as artificial, particularly as the language of instruction at first-year level is English.

> A 50-minute lecture is not long enough. I don't hear te reo – but we hear te reo Pākehā. I can't talk to a *tape*!

It's all too fast – you've got to get your money's worth. There's not enough time spent on the units . . . the lecturer will ask me 'have you got it yet?' I say 'No!' She says 'You can do it!' I say 'No I can't!'

In addition to the challenges of learning a language at a tertiary institution, many focus group participants came to university with limited ability to read effectively. For Mahara this was a result of leaving school at the age of 14.

The only book I had read was *Best Bets*!

Irihapeti, who had more secondary education, still had little idea how to read 'smart'.

We used to read textbooks cover to cover and then wonder why we got headaches!

Writing too continued to pose difficulties for many of the focus group members, particularly the structured writing required for essays. Simon expressed a belief that he has long held about his own abilities.

Māori are good with hands and eyes but not with pen and paper.

Mereraina expressed frustration over the time and effort it has taken her to learn the skills of academic writing.

I get in trouble with writing – getting how I think down on paper. There is no set method on how to write essays – but how are you supposed to put the information together? It is the same problem for essays in Māori. Structures for essays are hard.

Being left behind

For some of the students in the group, learning te reo and tikanga at a tertiary institution has been a confusing and at times painful experience. Irihapeti described coming through university with a small group of older Māori women who felt burdened because other people anticipated that they would achieve good grades and fulfil academic and cultural expectations. In a very real sense, these women became whānau for each other. Over the years many of these women became sick and died, leaving Irihapeti more isolated and wondering about her own cultural identity and the priorities set by a tertiary institution.

I had taken on board a lot of negative stuff about being Māori and I had to get As. Nothing else would do. But we push ourselves so hard to get those As – is it worth it? I lost [my friends] one by one . . . and I felt like I was the only one left to tell their story.

For other students the experience of learning te reo and tikanga in the university environment has not been as painful, but still leaves them feeling confused, and at times isolated from the other students.

I'm different – they are all speaking structures at the wananga and I can't recognise the dialects they use.

I just nod when I'm supposed to shake my head 'no'!

Cultural competence

Mature Māori students may also find themselves expected to give advice and pass on the knowledge that they bring from their own tribal areas to other Māori students. For Mereraina this has led to some confusion about her own role as a student.

I haven't learnt anything new in tikanga. In some lectures, there is expectancy for you to give advice on certain tikanga – confusing. Are you a student or an adviser?

For older urban Māori students like Irihapeti making a mistake in tikanga or te reo and being told off for it by others at the university can be galling.

There's a lot of fear: I'm never going to be a 'real Māori' with a marae base – I'm just a 'plastic born again'. There was no one [in the past] to tell me what is right and wrong – so when I get told off now – it's like a stake to the heart – but I'm starting to feel relaxed.

Some older Māori students may at times find themselves being corrected or pulled up by younger Māori. This can be difficult to accept, because older Māori students are expected to know more than younger students do.

Ngā hau e whā

The Māori population base in Wellington is very diverse. The iwi most represented in Wellington are from the East Coast of the North Island (Ngāti Porou and Ngāti Kahungunu). Also well represented are iwi from the Hawkes Bay, the Wairarapa, North Auckland and Northland, Bay of Plenty and Te Arawa/Taupo, among many others. Thus acclimatising to the pan-tribal nature of the university marae, Te Herenga Waka, is, in itself, a learning challenge that differs according to the cultural experiences of the mature student.

> Learning to do the pōwhiri and the karanga and working in the kitchen, for us not raised in Māori community, is really difficult.

> It helps you reflect on the past – sitting in on pōwhiri takes you back to being at home – studying and listening to those fullas on the paepae is really helpful

Mahara also acknowledged that the pan-tribal nature of Te Herenga Waka Marae enables him to be exposed to dialects and practices that he has not experienced before.

> Being at university taught me to recognise someone without knowing their name, just by their dialect and by just listening to them.

This exposure also helped Mahara overcome some of his whakamā about his own hapū background and resolve some long-standing issues of the past.

> A big source of embarrassment is where I'm from – there has been incestuous behaviour in our hapū and I just shut up about it until someone told me that that has happened *everywhere*. That was a huge relief.

Mereraina found that she has had to let go of some of her long-held conceptions about the nature of Māori identity. Through studying at Victoria University she met urban Māori mature students who have no marae other than that of the university to identify with.

> You look at a Māori and the first thought is that it all goes back to a marae but it's not always like that . . . and I have to stand back and be sensitive to other experiences I see. That's how I've been raised and I assume that's how it is for others – I take it for granted.

Many of the students in the focus group questioned some of the tikanga being taught at university. Much of that knowledge came from the tribal areas of their various lecturers and the students wondered how to repay their iwi for the knowledge that has been given. Mereraina and Miriam, in particular, expressed concern about how such Māori knowledge can be protected within tertiary institutions.[5]

> What protects our Māori things from being taken over? These things becomes the property of the university not of Māori.

> It's like selling your soul.

Conclusion

Māori students over the age of 35 are participating in tertiary education at higher rates than their non-Māori counterparts. In the 'Closing the Gaps' report this area was one of the very few where the disparity between Māori and non-Māori is in favour of the Māori population. The discussions held with the eight members of the focus group revealed that, for these students, university education reflects cultural goals that appear to be every bit as important as goals centred on career improvement or notions of self-improvement through education. All group participants acknowledged their roles as the bearers of knowledge to other members of their whānau and to people outside their whānau. In this sense, tertiary education was seen to be as much a collective good as a good accruing to the individual.

For the women of the group a significant aspect of their experience related to other people's perceptions of their achievements. Some showed concern lest they be viewed as better than other members of their whānau, particularly those who had not participated in tertiary education. For at least one member of the group her concern was not to denigrate the mana of her high-profile whānau. While the men of the group may well have felt the same anxieties about other people's perceptions, they voiced less concern on the matter and were more likely to speak positively of their achievements and of receiving positive reinforcement by other whānau members.

In line with the close connection between the participants and their whānau, and because all group participants were parents, and most were grandparents, it is not surprising that many saw whānau responsibilities as one of the biggest barrier to effective participation in university life and work. Also of major concern to some in the group was ongoing concern about a lack of practical skills such as academic reading and structured writing. There was little direct criticism of teaching staff except in the matter of the speediness of the lectures. A few of the mature students in the group felt 'left behind' by the pace of the teaching.

Most negative comments about the university were made in the context of criticising the structured lecture-based system as inappropriate for the effective transmission of Māori language lessons and tikanga. However, when asked what they would do to change their learning experiences none of the group participants indicated that they intended to change their approach to their own learning. Instead they offered some suggestions for better communication; for example being able to speak to other mature students with similar needs and experiences would have been very helpful.

Almost all group members acknowledged that they wanted to attend university either to attain knowledge about tikanga and/or reo that had either been denied them in earlier years or to recover such knowledge that had been lost, largely due to the compulsory education system. At the same time as seeking to shore up their own knowledge of the Māori language and cultural practices, most of the students had also found themselves, as older Māori, expected to be culturally competent and advise other younger students in the very areas they were seeking knowledge in. This has led to some confusion for the older people in understanding their roles as students in the university system.

All group members acknowledged the irony of attending a Pākehā tertiary institution to learn about their reo and tikanga. Despite this recognition, most reported that their learning experiences had been very positive. Only one woman stated explicitly that she had not learnt any new tikanga since her arrival at the university. Several members of the group also expressed concern about the university owning the information their lecturers had taught them.

Through the focus group process, it became clear that the students who took part had started out with some preconceptions of the experiences of other mature Māori students. Those who had more exposure to things Māori found that they appreciated learning more of the experiences other students who had not had the same cultural upbringing. By the same token, the students who felt less secure in their own cultural identities found that some of their experiences were not so very different from those more culturally experienced students. All members of the group at the end of their time together expressed a wish that they had had the chance to talk over these issues earlier in their university careers.

He mihi aroha

Ka nui ngā mihi ki a koutou ngā manu kōrero, nā koutou enei kōrero i tū ai te kaupapa. Ka nui ngā mihi hoki ki a Te Ripowai Higgins te kai whakahaere o te rōpū nei, ki a Tākuta Susan Gee hoki, nāna tēnei kaupapa i tautoko.

Glossary

hapū	subtribe
iwi	tribe/people
karanga	formal ritual calls made by women on the marae
kōrero	talk
mana	social standing
marae	a formal gathering place/space for Māori. Traditionally included an ancestral house, dining space and other associated areas
maunga	mountain
paepae	group of male speakers for formal rituals on the marae
pōwhiri	welcome ceremony
reo	language, the Māori language
tikanga	cultural knowledge
wānanga	Māori tertiary education institution
whakamā	self-effacement, embarrassment, shame
whānau	extended family

Notes

1 For example, the survey records that the most popular major for Māori students was education. However, only one of the eight focus group members was enrolled in education papers.

2 Te Puni Kokiri (2000) p.20.

3 The participants have all been given pseudonyms to protect confidentiality.

4 Durie et al (1996).

5 For a discussion on this issue see Durie (1998) pp.75–9.

5

IS IT WORTH IT? – FULL-TIME TEACHERS WHO STUDY AT UNIVERSITY PART-TIME

Kay Morris Matthews

What is it about teachers over forty? Why do they put themselves through such a tough regime over a number of years so at the end they can walk away with a first, second or even third university qualification? Is it not enough that they already hold a basic qualification to enable them to teach in the first place? Is it not enough that they teach classrooms of children for six hours a day, prepare or assess work for at least another ten hours a week, attend meetings and coach sports teams? What about their personal life commitments? Is it not enough they then go home to families with all their demands? Run households? Do the shopping? Have a life? How then do they manage to do justice to all of the above *and* be a part-time university student? This paper addresses both the reasons and the dynamics associated with the experiences of New Zealand teachers who are also part-time university students. It also assesses whether or not the teachers who took part in this research, and who have now graduated, thought all the effort and stress worth it in the end.

New Zealand universities have encouraged mature students to enroll for degree study and in the case of teachers have emphasised the importance of doing so in terms of professional development. In New Zealand, as in the United Kingdom, recent statistics indicate that education is the leading subject area for mature university students in social sciences and humanities and that the majority of these students are women.[1]

Despite this, there is little research on teachers as university students, either in terms of professional education or their experiences as mature students. I would argue that it is only when schools of education better understand how the courses they offer are actually experienced by full-time teachers that it becomes possible to develop better policy, curricula and teaching practice for this significant group of their students.

This idea is evident in recent publications relating to aspects of teachers' lives. Sue Middleton and Helen May, for example, lay down a challenge to educational researchers to think about teachers in a variety of ways and encourage the use of a 'wide-angled lens'. This is so that 'teachers are not viewed as passive recipients of the ideas of policy makers or the latest theoretical fashion, but as creative strategists whose theories-in-practice are products of their own agency'.[2] This makes good sense when considering teachers taking up university study later in life.

While the professional interface with learning is important, so too are other considerations. Educational researchers, such as Sue Middleton and Kathleen Weiler,[3] remind us that we can look at the ways in which teachers are defined by the institutions in which they work and study, but we need also to look at the ways in which teachers define themselves.

The majority of mature teachers who study part-time are women and one can only stand back and marvel at the necessary organisational and management strategies they need to employ in order to cope with their multiple-layered lives. These layers include their lives as teacher professionals with all that entails, such as teaching preparation, classroom management, pupil assessment, curriculum development, peer review and parent liaison. But the layers of 'otherness', as student and family member, means having to travel to university after school in order to be a student, the allocation of study time plus childcare and elderly parent care as well as ongoing domestic and community responsibilities.

There is a reasonable amount of literature on adult or mature students who take up education at university in mid and later life. In the main, this research includes such topics as motivation to study, access,[4] achievement and academic performance,[5] institutional barriers and/or innovations,[6] gender and fields of study[7] and student perceptions of the education experience.[8] There is little literature on part-time university students in general[9] or on part-time students who are teachers.[10] However, as Turner and Bash[11] point out, regarding British teachers, it is important to recognise a number of factors affecting professional development. Particularly, 'given that study for advanced qualifications is mostly undertaken on a part-time basis, [it] can be interrupted as a result of work and domestic considerations and thus, undertaken at a much later date'.

The context and mature students

The larger study, of which this paper is part, examines the situation of people in mid and later life who are taking up educational opportunities. Education was by far the most popular subject for mature students at Victoria University. Eighty-six teachers answered the postal questionnaire. All worked full-time in early childhood centres, primary schools, intermediate schools, secondary schools, polytechnics, and colleges of education, or were curriculum advisors in schools. They were located predominantly in the Wellington area, although a number were distance students based in schools in the South Island. All studied part-time at Victoria University and graduated either in 1999 or in 2000. Of the total, around a quarter (22) were interviewed and data for this chapter is drawn from both the postal questionnaire and interview material.

Demographic profile of teachers aged 40 and over
Of the 86 teachers, the majority (64%) were aged between 40 and 49. A further 31% were aged between 50 and 59. The group comprised mainly Pākehā/European (81%) with 9% identifying as Māori. A large percentage (84%) of this group were women. All those studying at undergraduate level (10) were women, 27 out of 32 postgraduate diploma students were women, and also 20 out of a total of 29 Masters students. A comparable analysis of older graduates conducted by Graham in Britain[12] also showed that the number of women studying education greatly exceeded men. This may simply reflect the higher proportion of women in the teaching profession generally. Or it may be because women have recognised that the key to career advancement within teaching, or a way out of teaching, is advanced qualifications.

At the time of the study, 10% of all the teachers were working in early childhood education, while 65% were teaching in the primary school area and 3% were secondary school teachers. Nearly a quarter of this group taught in polytechnics, colleges of education or were curriculum advisors. This reflects the growing trend for staff at polytechnics and colleges of education to obtain at least Master's degree level qualifications.

The survey asked about the teachers' living situations. Half of the respondents were living with their partner and adult/dependent children while 5% were raising children on their own. One quarter were living with their partner only, while 10% lived alone and 7% lived in extended family households.

Teachers were also asked about their personal and household incomes. Sixty-five percent stated that their personal incomes were between $40,001 and $70,000. When household incomes were considered, 46.5% indicated that this was $70,001 or more. Conversely, only 8.1% had a household income of between $20,000 and $30,000. This reflects comparatively high incomes among the postal survey respondents as a whole. When asked about funding difficulties associated with study, 52% did not answer and 24% indicated they had no difficulties with funding their study. However, teachers who were also sole parents with children living at home frequently cited financial difficulties as a barrier to their continuing university study.

The motivation to study

For nearly one-third of the teachers, the most commonly cited trigger for deciding to study was compulsory training. That is, within areas such as early childhood and special needs education, the Ministry of Education has issued an edict that if teachers want to continue to be employed they have to upgrade their qualifications within a certain period of time. This level of compulsion reflects the high proportion of teacher respondents studying for a Diploma of Special Needs Resource Teaching (Dip.SNRT). The second most commonly cited trigger for deciding to study was reduced childcare responsibilities.

Respondents were asked to rank five different motivations for their decision to return or begin study. 'Acquiring new knowledge or qualifications for improving job performance or prospects' was the most highly ranked by 21% of the teachers. Next came personal development and fulfillment (13%) followed by compulsory training (7%) and work-related change/redundancy (6%). This ranking of motivations mirrors Bourner's et al[13] British study of part-time university students. This indicated that the major motivation to undertake part-time study was to improve career prospects. In the New Zealand study this point is clearly demonstrated. For example, a college of education lecturer became increasingly aware that 'I was one of the last people employed at college without a degree' and set out to get one both for reasons of parity and job security. Another experienced teacher with an undergraduate diploma and who was director of an early childhood centre could see that 'teachers were coming out with a Bachelor of Education and if I was to continue managing the centre, I had to have a higher qualification'. As a solo parent, financing study was particularly difficult and it was only after several years saving that she enrolled to complete a first degree. Part-time study proved too difficult so she decided 'to go back on to the benefit and to take out a student loan' so that she could become a full-time student. At the point of interview, she was about to graduate with a Master's in Education.

The women teachers in this New Zealand study associated higher education and qualifications with being taken more seriously at work, giving them more status and prestige both as paid workers and as mothers/partners. This is contrary to a popular stereotype that women return to education because of dissatisfaction with family lives. Rather, the women teachers were clear that their return to study was motivated by the realisation that they did not want to spend the remainder of their teaching lives in jobs that they found to be unsatisfying both in terms of personal and monetary rewards. Combining part-time study with full-time teaching may be tough but it is, many women teachers told us, the way to gain a promotional edge in the longer term. These findings are consistent with Edwards's British study of mature women students, where 75% of those surveyed cited future job prospects and career advancement as key motivating factors in their decision to return to university study.[14]

Study choices and experiences
A large number of respondents provided their educational biographies revealing interesting career pathways. Upon leaving school, often with endorsed School Certificate and a negative view of secondary schooling, many of the women teachers took up secretarial training, as was common in the late 1960s and early 1970s for women without higher school qualifications. Many worked in a range of office situations but upon marriage, spent a number of years at home bearing and rearing children. In the later 1970s, many responded to the call for teacher trainees, completed teacher training and took up full-time teaching. Some years later, they realised that to advance in teaching they now required a degree and as students over forty years of age, embarked upon university study. To do so, however, was not straightforward. There were issues of confidence, self-esteem and a sense of entering alien territory. A primary

teacher completing a Bachelor of Arts in education reflected that 'during my own education as working class, I had no role models for university work'. Another teacher, completing a Bachelor of Early Childhood Education said, 'Since leaving school I believed that I was too "dumb" to go to university. I had to work through that emotional response before I could start.'

Of the teachers in this study, only ten were undergraduates, half of whom were enrolled in a Bachelor of Arts degree and the other half in a Bachelor of Education degree. Of the remainder, the highest numbers were enrolled in a Postgraduate Diploma in Special Needs Resource Teaching followed closely by those enrolled in a Master of Education. Others were enrolled in a Postgraduate Diploma in Education Studies, Master of Arts, Master of Public Policy, Master of Communications, Master of Library and Information Studies and Master of Developmental Studies. Two were enrolled for a Doctor of Philosophy.

Keeping the study motivation going
Given the reasons for studying, does the fact that they are twice as old as the average university student affect their study in any way? Like the students aged 60 and over (see chapter nine), a high proportion of teachers (87%) believed that there were advantages in being a student over 40, with 31% citing general life experience giving them an edge as a student. Motivation/focus (30%) and confidence/maturity (23%) were given as the personal advantages. That is, respondents often commented that as older students they had spent years learning how to prioritise a number of tasks, with the women in particular citing the combination of work and home commitments. Although this did not necessarily remove the stress factors once study was added in, as a group many believed it gave them an edge.

The motivation to learn rather than merely pass papers, was a comparison some made with study experiences when younger. In the main, this was associated with a more focused course of study, which, in the majority of cases, was directly applicable to their professional goals and interests. Such motivation is also significant for nurses as discussed in chapter six. Other kinds of comparisons were also made by the teachers. Firstly, as an older student one was 'more inclined to get on with the study' rather than being sidetracked by student politics or romance. A woman primary teacher completing a Master's degree put it this way. 'I know what I want. I am at university to study, not socialise. I am committed to seeing it through.' A great number thought that confidence and maturity meant that they were more able to speak with university staff about their concerns or seek help. As one teacher put it, 'I'm not as scared to say I don't understand.'

Time and experience
This confidence is placed in context when the age and career span of the teachers is considered. About a third had taught full-time for 5 to 15 years, but the majority (66%) were very experienced teachers and had taught for more than 15 years. Of these, 19 had taught full-time for more than 20 years, while four had taught full-time for between 30 and 34 years and of these, two had 32 years continuous service.

These very experienced teachers, then, wanted a new qualification but were generally resigned to the fact that it had taken a long time to complete. That is, over one-third of the teachers had taken between three and five years to complete a degree part-time, while a further 15% had spent more than five years on a qualification. This would be expected with an undergraduate degree, with all teachers in this category taking three years or more. However, what was interesting is that those enrolled in a Master of Education degree had usually taken longer, with all 21 teachers taking three years or more and seven taking more than five years.

For some women, it had been a long hard road interrupted by marriage breakdown, financial concerns and the balancing of work and study with childcare. As a primary teacher of 19 years summed it up, she had first thought of studying at university when she embarked upon primary teaching training in 1979. By the time she enrolled six years later, she was separated from her husband and saw a tertiary qualification as the way to 'widen my job opportunities' and to improve her future income. Sixteen years later, she graduated with a Bachelor of Arts, majoring in linguistics. Another had taken 18 years to complete a Bachelor of Arts. Now in her 50s, she reflected that she had taught and supported her daughters through university. Once they had graduated, she decided to complete her own degree.

Conversely, there were a number of teachers who studied part-time yet had completed advanced qualifications in a relatively short time frame despite numerous difficulties along the way. A woman secondary school teacher in her 50s, for example, took four years to complete a Master of Education while raising two children on her own. As an older Māori woman she was clear that while her primary motivating factor to return to study was to acquire new knowledge, the second most important was to set an example to her children. In 1966, she left secondary school with endorsed School Certificate and undertook secretarial studies at polytechnic. Some years later, she embarked upon a teacher training course before completing a Bachelor of Arts part-time. Now that she has also completed a Master's degree, she is contemplating enrolling for a doctorate.

Being a student
Although as a group the teachers in this study often coped with enormous stress, they were intent on completing a qualification. Perhaps because of their professional training, they were also forthright about their study experience, both good and bad. Many mentioned positive factors related to 'being in a university atmosphere', 'contact with other teachers' and a genuine enjoyment of the lecture/seminar sessions. Intellectual stimulation therefore was an important aspect of being a university student.

One woman teacher completing an undergraduate degree said –

> I find it really exciting and it has nothing to do with work . . . I love sitting in the lectures and I love the actual campus environment. I love the buzz of it. Whenever I'm grumpy about university I come and have a tutorial and I always leave feeling better . . . I love that whole buzz of learning things.

In reflecting upon their own personal qualities, the older students thought the most difficult barrier was to learn and perform as a student. That is, many expressed doubts about their ability to cope with academic work, although closer questioning revealed above average grades for course work. Surprisingly, perceived lack of confidence associated with study was cited more often than lower energy levels to cope with home, work and study. As had been mentioned earlier, a range of factors in the lives of teachers over forty who study part-time all point to such teachers being in the 'superhuman' category when it comes to energy levels. This is further demonstrated by one teacher with three teenage children. Recently appointed to a new position as head of department she estimated that she was spending on average 50 hours at work a week. Completing a Master of Arts, she concluded,

> I would like to be a full-time student in order to have achieved As of which I am capable. Family and work demands led me to be satisfied with lesser marks. Also just to have the time to *fully* focus would have been great, especially without working late at nights, and being fresher in the day.

Being realistic about what it was possible to achieve was a common theme, especially given the high work commitment. Many teachers mentioned disappointment with attaining anything less than an A grade, but one senior teacher completing a Master's degree and reflecting on just how stressful it had been, recommended that in order to achieve the overall goal 'don't get poisoned with perfection'.

The good times and the bad

However, university study was particularly enjoyable for the teachers because of the intellectual challenges. Many academic staff were singled out for special mention, both for their subject expertise but also because they had stimulated students to think in different ways and to read widely. School of education staff were particularly praised. A male school principal put it like this –

> I really liked the ideas and the information and being up with current thinking and the access to current and challenging thinking. That to me was the most valuable part.

All teachers interviewed stressed the importance of meeting other students and the collegiality –

> We have all become friends and some of us still socialise.

> It's not just learning, it's making friendships. It is about study groups in the Astoria Café and talking about post-structuralism . . . that's just priceless to me. It's like a whole opening up.

Some teachers completing their degrees were also critical about their experience of university study. While there were few concerns about course content, there were complaints about poor lecturing, such as, 'my time is pressed – it has to be worthwhile', 'when you pay big fees and your time is precious, you don't expect that'. Other criticisms were of poor organisation of material, types of assignment, pressure of assignments and interestingly, the competitiveness of fellow students. A major theme that emerged was the structural isolation that many experienced, especially as teachers undertaking postgraduate study. While not being able to find a staff member to talk with out of class time may be a common complaint, teachers thought that there were 'too many assumptions made that we will know our way around and know what to do and who to talk to'. Other concerns included not being able to attend postgraduate student association seminars because they were held during the day as well as frustrations with obtaining new ID cards in order to access the library. Comparisons were also made with other universities where the perception was that 'graduates were wooed and properly looked after' with 24-hour access to computers and workrooms with telephones. Having study rooms and facilities is essential for postgraduate students and this fact is recognised by the school of education at Victoria University.[15]

Tough times
Although the demands of family life place a strain on work and student life, the teachers in this study thought that the demands of work were more of a disadvantage. This is clearly linked to the number of hours spent on schoolwork and the increasing pressures on teachers and school administrators to meet curriculum and assessment audit deadlines. When asked about the average number of hours each spent in paid work per week, 57% said they worked 40 hours or more, with 21% of these estimating it was more like 50–60 hours a week. The question is, how do teachers with this type of professional load cope with study, let alone family obligations as well?

Every teacher told me that it was 'difficult' and 'hard' and only manageable in the main if one abandoned any kind of a social life or recreational activities in order to spend time where it was needed. Both men and women found it difficult to juggle the competing demands of out-of-school time, that is the time left over from paid work, between family and study. While teachers cited the initial support of family members in returning to study, they reported that most family members found the period of sustained study very difficult indeed. Several reported that the strain placed upon their family life was intense.

Family life almost disintegrated at one stage (teacher with partner and two young children).

It was just an absolute nightmare. In the end I did not know if I was doing anything properly (teacher with partner and three young children).

My marriage would not have survived if I had not finished [the qualification] when I did (teacher with partner and three adolescents).

A male primary teacher who was completing a Master of Education degree while bringing up three children under ten years of age provides a graphic example. At work, he averaged up to 60 hours per week. His partner worked 35 hours a week. Although the study experience had been as he expected, it was 'extremely difficult to accommodate work, family and study commitments'. Not surprisingly, what he viewed as the major barrier to his study was 'Time! Time! Time!'

Work and study plus young children
For those with young children, adequate childcare in after-school hours remained a perennial problem. While teachers generally appreciated that courses were offered in after-school hours, often beginning at 4 or 5pm, there was always a dilemma about leaving children until their partner returned from work. In New Zealand in the year 2000, the average age at which a woman has her first baby is 29.[16] Hence, while some mature students are returning to study because they have completed family care, for many continuing responsibility for children living at home is their reality. This was the case for an early childhood teacher whose 11- and 7-year-old children required regular childcare over the two years it took her to compete her undergraduate degree. She cited the two main barriers to achieving her goal as obtaining regular childcare and tiredness.

Most interviewees mentioned the ever present 'tiredness' summed up by a senior woman teacher with children living at home.

It required constant adherence to a strict timetable, time management skills became a game of survival. *No* time wastage. Strict priorities! I would keep the vision of the end goal; work during the night to avoid interruption – from 2–5am.

The teachers with children living at home consistently reported that full-time teaching and part-time study required an understanding partner and/or children. With the pressure of completing assignments combined with a busy work life, most reported not having too much time left for anything else.

It was demanding for my family. They missed out on having me for more of the time and often, when I was around, the stress levels were high. They had to do more, which was not necessarily a bad thing, but they resented it a bit.

Sole parenting, work and study
While undertaking part-time study with a supportive partner remains a challenge, completing a degree as a solo parent brings its own additional worries. A secondary teacher completing a Master of Education degree commented on –

the multiple layers of commitment required to raise my son and daughter and ongoing and hidden costs related to juggling family commitments and study.

Among these were the travelling costs associated with the 20 miles return trip into classes, and for regular babysitters at home. Another sole parent had spent the past three years completing an undergraduate degree while working in the early childhood sector. Her children were now aged 15, 13 and 10, but the three years had meant, 'stress due to the demands of my life as a single parent on a low income'. This was because her early childhood teacher's salary was insufficient to support her family and she had taken on additional paid work. However, she had been forced to reduce the extra work during the period of study in order 'to do justice to everything'. Despite the stress, which she emphasised several times, she was pleased to have completed a degree and encouraged others over 40 years of age who were considering a return to study, saying 'you can do it too'.

The demands of children were frequently mentioned, but so too were the increasing demands of older parents. The 'sandwich generation'- the baby boomers that had their children later in life – may now find they have younger children and older parents to provide support for at the same time. A teacher writing her Master's thesis was an example of this. She spoke of the time when a parent became ill and required regular care, adding to her responsibilities as a mother with two children living at home. Another Master's student wrote of the reasons why she had been enrolled in the same degree for 11 years but was now about to complete it. 'Issues of responsibility to family and friends' had meant that she had taken time out from her studies to care for her ill mother and ill husband in turn. She had also taken time out from teaching during this time and there had been occasions when she could not afford to pay the year's fees.

Is it worth it?
Many teachers did not, in fact, consider the university study experience worth the sacrifices made in respect to their family lives. Only one third offered unqualified encouragement to prospective older students and the rest were generally less enthusiastic about being mature students than other groups reported on in this book. The reasons for this include the considerable trials and tribulations associated with combining a full-time teaching job with part-time university study and the fact that a large proportion of this group were women. Many of the teachers interviewed were obliged to take on the extra study and this may also have given them a less than positive impression of the university experience.

Advice to teachers contemplating university study
Many teachers, however, were clear about what was needed in order to make the study experience worthwhile. Organisational and time management skills were high on the list. One woman deputy-principal who estimated she worked 60–65 hours a week at school while completing a Master of Education offered this advice.

> Organise your time very carefully and always make a commitment to do the work each week. Give yourself some time out during the year to relax. Otherwise, you'll burn out if you are in full-time work.

Having a 'buddy' was also critical to making the study experience 'worth it'. Many teachers cited the importance of 'having a study buddy' and the particular advantage associated with support from an immediate colleague doing the same degree – 'It was great having a colleague to interact with and discuss lectures and assignments with.' Many part-time students do not have the luxury that full-time students have, of time to forge friendships on campus or the possibility of meeting to discuss course content over lunch in the cafeteria, for example.

Other necessities were recommended. For example, a full-time teacher who was married with five children living at home offered practical advice – 'give up sex and cooking'. The demands of family are clearly reflected in many of the responses. Working an average of 60 hours a week, one primary teacher with teenage children advised, 'get a housekeeper, a gardener and a taxi driver to transport the children.' Others too, had learnt that part-time study required a certain state of mind. For example, an MA student in her fifties advised – 'Be ruthless, put yourself first.'

In regard to their futures, teachers were asked about the likely effect of gaining a university degree or qualification. Eighty-four percent believed that the degree would have a very positive or positive effect on their careers in terms of promotion or opening up new possibilities, although only 58% thought that their salary would improve as a result. Of the recent graduates 62% thought that their current or recently completed studies had improved the likelihood of their undertaking further study.

Satisfaction and completion

For those interviewed who had completed the qualification, there was overwhelming pride as well as a measure of disbelief that the goal had finally been achieved. For all, it was very important to finish but having done so, most do not want to study formally again. 'I don't want any more stress, especially if I move into being a principal.' Reflecting on gains other than promotion, many emphasised that the qualification made a difference in how colleagues and family members viewed them. One woman teacher remarked – 'I became more focused, more confident, more sure of my own ideas and this has affected my confidence both at work and home.'

Like many of the mature students reported in this book, there were teachers for whom the university study experience meant a great deal.

I think it's given me a hell of a lot of confidence in all sorts of ways. I think it has been good as a dad to do so. My two daughters can see that I value that, because I grew up with parents who did not value tertiary education. As a principal of a decile ten school, quite a few parents are well educated and its given me the confidence to deal with them more equally – they can see that I can actually run a school really effectively and efficiently and get good results' (male school Principal, with newly completed Master of Education).

I realise that I *am* intellectually able, and I no longer have these feelings of inadequacy when I talk to people who are bright or well qualified (female teacher with newly completed Master of Education).

Having the Master's has given more credibility and a lot more confidence in dealing with people like ERO [Education Review Office] and the Ministry. Having the Master's is really important (male school Principal with newly completed MBA).

It is significant that it is the male teachers who spoke at length about the positive outcomes of their university study as mature students. This could be for a number of reasons including recent career success as a result of gaining the qualification. By their own admission, those with families benefited because their partners had taken on extra domestic and parenting tasks to compensate for the other partners' study. However, while the women teachers appreciated any sharing of domestic and parenting tasks by their partners, they clearly believed that they retained and in many cases, should retain, the major responsibility for running the home.

It is not surprising therefore, that teachers who work full-time and study part-time over a number of years and who are also older, get tired, stressed and wonder if it is worthwhile. For those who persevere, the completion of a qualification, followed by graduation, is greeted with a huge sigh of relief – a goal achieved.

I just feel a sense of completion and it is probably doesn't matter to anyone else in the world except me, that I have actually done it. There are a lot of people with a Bachelor of Arts but the fact that I've actually done it, graduated, worn the gown and all the pomp and ceremony has been quite important as well (female primary school teacher, after seven years study).

I just feel as though there is a huge part of my brain that's suddenly relaxed and not filled up any more . . . I have this wonderful sense of going out to do some practical art for myself, of doing things, of having a social life. It's so different waking up in the morning in the weekends and thinking I do not have to study. I can garden! (female Resource Teacher of Learning and Behaviour after two years study).

While recreation time has been reclaimed so too have professional lives, although with differing reactions. One teacher reflected, 'the quality of planning and thinking about schoolwork has improved immensely and that's a bit scary.' While for many this is certainly so, those teachers who had graduated were clearly missing the study aspect of their lives. As one woman deputy principal put it 'If I died now, they're going to put on my gravestone – died, because she was so bloody bored'. Another, who has gained a new school principalship since graduating, sensed he had got the balance back in his life through spending more time with his family.

> I'm more determined about how education in school needs to perform. I am more equipped to be more efficient and effective in education and in particular in schools. [The study] has influenced me as a person. I'm more critical thinking. It's sharpened, more analytical. Better tools to model things on and more determined than ever. And more. I have a better base to challenge what has happened or what people think.

So 'is it worth it' for full-time teachers to study part-time at university when they are 40 years and older? The answer was mixed. For 86 teachers in this study feelings of success were set alongside the sheer hard slog of the work/study combination. Both men and women teachers regretted the lack of time to spend with partners and children, but the majority, as women, reported that they had retained the major responsibility for home and family. That so many had children living at home is a significant feature of the research. Not surprisingly therefore, although university study was stimulating and in the main enjoyable, the overall reaction to it was clearly tempered with the everyday reality of finding time to do justice to professional, family and study demands.

Notes

1   Ministry of Education (2001).
2   Middleton and May (1997) p.10.
3   Middleton & Weiler (1999).
4   Leonard (1994).
5   Richardson (1995) pp.5–17.
6   James (1995) pp.451–66.
7   Edwards (1993).
8   Wilson (1997) pp.347–66.

9 Schuller, Raffe, Morgan-Klein and Clark (1999).

10 Thompson (1997).

11 Turner & Bash (1999).

12 Graham (1989).

13 Bourner, Hamed, Barnett and Reynolds (1988).

14 Edwards (1993).

15 The Victoria University school of education is currently housed in inadequate and temporary buildings and is forced to prioritise the study needs of its many doctoral students. In a bid to address similar concerns of postgraduate students right across the faculty of humanities and social sciences, a large computer room has been recently established and especially designated for their use.

16 Statistics New Zealand (2001) 'Births and Deaths'. Year ending September 2001. http://www.stats.govt.nz.

6

NURSES AT UNIVERSITY – NEGOTIATING ACADEMIC, WORK AND PERSONAL PATHWAYS

Allison Kirkman and Alison Dixon

Nursing and nurses are in the news these days. In the main this news is about the problems of recruitment and retention of qualified nurses. When the interviews for this chapter were carried out the newspaper headlines focused on the 'nursing shortage' in New Zealand and the 'brain drain' of qualified nurses and other health workers. As we write this chapter mediation is underway between Canterbury District Health Board and the nurses' union, New Zealand Nurses' Organisation (NZNO), to try and resolve a long-standing dispute over pay and conditions for nurses in Christchurch. This media focus on nurses and nursing is not surprising when we consider that nurses comprise the largest group of workers in the health workforce. Not only are they the largest group of workers, they are also a group with an ageing profile. In 2000, 59% of nurses with current practising certificates are between the ages of 40 and 59 years.[1] In view of this it seems particularly useful to explore the experiences of nurses who returned to study in mid or later life. We are particularly interested in the career trajectories and aspirations of nurses who gain tertiary qualifications other than their initial qualification for registration as a nurse. For instance, is the motivation to attend university related to advancing a nursing career or does it signal a change of career direction? Is university study related to personal goals or is it now a 'requirement' for promotion? And, if the latter, how does this university study influence nursing practice? These are some of the questions that we hoped to answer when we set out to complete this chapter.

Nurses and university study

This chapter draws upon two main sources of data: first, the profile of

96 people who indicated that a nursing qualification was their highest educational attainment in the 'Education in Mid and Later Life' postal survey, and second, in-depth interviews with 15 women selected from this larger group. We will first summarise the characteristics of the survey respondents to provide background to the in-depth interviews. Most of the respondents were in the 40–49 age group and 92 of the 96 were women. Only 6% of this group were Māori and 4% Pacific Nation people, while 83% identified as Pākehā. The majority were studying part-time (89%) and a significant number (66%) were also working 30 hours or more a week in paid employment.

In the group of 96, the majority of these respondents were living with a partner (74%) and over half (60%) had children still living at home. Overall, 59% were enrolled in nursing programmes and of these 56% were undertaking an MA (Applied), 23% an MA and 18% a postgraduate certificate in advanced nursing. Forty-one percent were doing programmes other than nursing, with nearly half doing a BA.

Interviewing nurses

The 15 women who participated in the interviews had indicated their willingness to participate on the initial postal questionnaire. The decision to restrict the in-depth interviews to women was because the majority of the nursing workforce comes into this gender group. In the group of 96 respondents only 4 were male and this parallels other available information on gender composition of nurses in New Zealand and elsewhere. For example, in the year 2000–2001 49,456 people had annual nursing practicing certificates in New Zealand, but only 2,744 of these were men. Interviewing women is also important because as Anne Witz put it 'the problem *for* nursing has been and continues to be the problem *of* gender'.[2] The identification of nursing work as caring work and therefore more 'naturally' female work will be explored later in this chapter.

However, another reason this group of nurses is particularly significant and warrants further attention is that their experiences are located at the cusp of the major change that occurred in nursing education in New Zealand. Up until 1973, nursing training in New Zealand was undertaken in hospitals in the form of the traditional apprenticeship model. This training occurred in different types of hospital schools of nursing and led to three forms of registration; general and obstetric, psychiatric and psychopaedic registration. Concerns about the quality of teaching and learning, the high rate of those not completing the training, and the lack of parity of nurses' education with that of other health professionals were well documented, and were commented on by all those interviewed –

> I think that the nursing training today equips young nurses to actually ask questions, to actually look at the way they're doing things; rather than doing things because someone tells them to. . . . I mean I can just think about when we were hospital trained, that we were almost treated like registered nurses and we would be the most senior nurse in the ward. We'd have a huge amount of responsibility. Looking back I think it was daft. I think it was terrible, and I mean I think that there were lots of things that went wrong there. But thinking of the nurses who are coming through [now] they're actually learning how to learn . . . I don't think they will get into the same worries that we got into (hospital trained psychiatric and general and obstetric nurse).[3]

The Carpenter Report in 1971 laid the foundation for the movement of nursing education from hospital training to the education sector. As a result of Helen Carpenter's recommendations and lobbying by nurses, preregistration nursing education was progressively transferred to the tertiary sector. By the late 1980s, undergraduate nursing education was established in 15 polytechnics. These nursing education programmes led to a Diploma in Nursing and registration as a New Zealand Comprehensive Nurse. This 'comprehensive' registration incorporated the three earlier forms of registration and enabled the beginning practitioner to work in any healthcare field. The notion of a comprehensive nursing education has remained pivotal to subsequent developments in nursing education, the most significant of which was the approval and accreditation of the first undergraduate preregistration nursing degrees by the New Zealand Qualifications Authority in 1992. While polytechnics offer these nursing degrees, three universities (Auckland University, Auckland University of Technology and Massey University) now offer undergraduate nursing degrees leading to comprehensive registration. Therefore for young women and men embarking on a nursing education in 2002 a degree programme is not unusual nor is it unheard of to undertake it at a university. This is a major difference between the undergraduate nursing students of today and the 15 women interviewed for this study. Fourteen of the 15 women who were interviewed had undertaken their initial nursing training within hospital schools of nursing either as enrolled nurses, registered general and obstetric nurses or psychiatric nurses. Of the four who commenced with enrolled nurse training, three had then undertaken three-year programmes to register as either General and Obstetric Nurses (RGON) or Comprehensive Nurses (RCpN). Two had studied further to become Registered Midwives, and several had completed other post-basic courses such as a Plunket Certificate, Cardiothoracic Nursing Certificate, while five had completed BA degrees and a further two had papers toward their BA degrees. These were, therefore, a group of women accustomed to study and are examples of the current emphasis within nursing on lifelong learning. One woman put it well when she said –

> Well, there's this feeling that you've got to be showing that you are continuing in, in education, in everything nowadays (hospital trained psychiatric nurse).

This theme of 'continuing in education' was a major theme throughout the interviews but what does 'continuing in education' entail? In the next section we explore some of the reasons for nurses continuing with education and also the type of education undertaken. But first it is essential to explore further the gendered nature of nursing as an occupation. For the women interviewed in this study the range of occupations available to them when leaving school was more limited than today. What is known as vertical occupational segregation was a major characteristic of women's employment, and while this still exists today with women concentrated in three main occupational categories, this concentration into female-dominated occupations was even greater when these women left school and entered the workforce. The careers available at this time were teaching, nursing and clerical work. University study was the province of an elite small group of women from middle-class backgrounds.

> Nobody went (nursing). In fact I was ridiculed at the time. I went to a grammar school in England, and when I told them I wanted to go

nursing they, the teachers were in disgust, they said 'well you may as well not carry on with your A Level programme at all is if that's all you want to do. Don't need A Levels to be a nurse.' Yes and they were quite sort of, it's almost like they brush you aside, if you didn't want to do, go to university or polytech or next one down was teaching and almost in that order. Then ah, there was no point in being at a grammar school you could have gone through secondary modern system and that was really their attitude. So my parents didn't think nursing would be a good thing for me to do at all. Ah, they said it was hard work and I couldn't understand why because all these people in the soap opera running around chasing handsome doctors (laughs) and giving out pills, and that's all they seemed to be doing. And I thought it looked very glamorous (laughs) (hospital trained general nurse).

Sue Middleton's work, using case studies to explore school experiences of girls in New Zealand in the 1950s and 1960s, illustrates the ways in which the organisation of schools through 'streaming' influenced girls' perceptions of femininity and appropriate models of womanhood.[4] Within the top streams, girls of predominantly middle-class backgrounds developed intellectual subcultures 'based on a virginal model of female sexuality' and a 'model of intellectuality' based on fantasies about 'academic/artistic bohemia'. 'Bright' girls turned away from nursing which was often seen as the 'soft option'.[5]

And as one woman said about her decision to go nursing 'my father wasn't very pleased about that, even though his sister was a nurse. Because he was working at the university and thought I ought to go to university because we could.'

Nursing was frequently seen as practical work and practical work was separate from intellectual work. This practical work was based on the qualities associated with being female – that of being nurturing and caring – and because they were 'natural' qualities they needed harnessing rather than education to bring them into fruition. Nurses, in fact, were born not made.

I always felt from the time I could remember I always wanted to be a nurse. I was raised with my grandparents and I can remember looking after sick animals and pets. So it just sort of seemed natural that that's where I was heading (hospital trained general nurse).

This perception that nurses did not need to be intellectually bright, not unexpectedly, had been internalised by some of the respondents and is reflected in their attempts to justify why they are nurses. One example of this is where respondents pointed out that they could have done medicine but were not permitted for a variety of reasons. These reasons included the traditional careers expected of girls by parents –

> Well I wanted to be a doctor you see. [Interviewer – Did you?] But my father didn't think it was like, you know, for us. You're just a girl. [Interviewer – mm, mm, mm.] You're just a girl (hospital trained general nurse).

and by school counsellors at this time –

> what I had been interested in was being a doctor but the school guidance counsellor dissuaded me from that direction by telling me that I would get married and have children and it would be a waste of the taxpayers' money. And when I protested that I wouldn't be getting married and having children he eventually implied that I didn't have the intelligence anyway, so . . . (hospital trained psychiatric nurse).

The influence of this distinction between medicine as intellectual and nursing as practical was not lost on some of these women, and one who has a higher degree in nursing made the comment:

> I think you have to be careful that you don't make it more than it is . . . it is, nursing is nursing you know, it's not medicine and it's not something else, it's nursing and that involves a lot of basic care for people's bodies when they're sick. You know, as well as all the nice primary health care stuff and education roles and all that. But really if you were whittling nursing services right down the one thing you would still keep, I'm sure, is nurses working in an acute care area. And so you've got to recognise it, the job for what it is (hospital trained general and obstetric nurse, PhD).

However, the more general anti-intellectual stance to nursing can be an obstacle to further education as one woman found in her practice nursing work when it was suggested by one of the doctors that practice nurses only need to be able to answer the phone politely –

> And they (the doctors) told me practice nurses don't need a degree and you definitely don't need a degree in something other than

nursing because if you do that its not nurse related so why should we give you time off. So I had to change my career. It's – you know – change from practice nursing and go. I thought well what else can I do, I'll have to go casual. I really didn't have a lot of choices, at least then I can pick my shifts.

This then is a tension for nurses and the tertiary education providers, like universities and polytechnics. On the one hand further education may enrich the individual nurse's life but does it benefit nursing practice more generally? To answer this question we will explore how the women in this study came to university studies.

Earlier educational experiences were pivotal

All the women interviewed had an understanding of the differences between a training and an education, and while many of them enjoyed their nursing training they were also aware of how it could have been different, and would be different if they were doing it today:

> I enjoyed my nursing, I enjoyed the hospital training. Well some parts of it I didn't enjoy. Because sometimes you were looking after things that you didn't actually know all that well, and you sort of got the education a bit later, when it would have been better to have got the education first and know a bit more about it (hospital trained general nurse).

> I do look back now in envy really at the nurses today, you know and the education they get. I mean I don't know it in detail but I know that it is a lot better than what we got (hospital trained psychiatric nurse).

Because the introduction of the polytechnic nursing programmes had been controversial, many of the women seemed to have thought through their ideas about education, and thinking about entering university was not such a major leap but rather part of a process that commenced with their initial nursing education and was still ongoing.

Some of the women had experienced a number of different programmes within universities and that first contact had an impact on the direction that their later studies took.

> I can remember when I first went to university because I'd never

been before. It was a business study one as well I think, and I walked into this lecture theatre and I'd never been in a lecture theatre ever, and I walked in and it was just, something like 300 people and I can remember looking in and I thought, oh my god. And I was by myself and I thought what, what am I doing here. And I can remember getting in and squeezing in one of those rows and I thought I've got to get out of here. And I just got up and left and I left the whole paper and I never went back and I sat outside crying, eating this apple thinking, this is stupid I'm an adult, (laughs). And I couldn't believe how it was, I didn't expect it to be like it, to be like that. I had this thing that we'd have classrooms, small ones but it was just so different.

This experience is probably not uncommon for women returning to study and attending large first-year classes. The most negative comments in interviews were made about these large first-year classes. As a consequence of this experience this woman did further study at a polytechnic before enrolling in an MA in nursing. This pathway ensured that she was in smaller classes with more interaction. As she says –

I enjoy the interaction with the other students in the class more than anything. I think it's good. I enjoy sometimes listening when you hear some of the lecturers talking, discussing across the classroom and things like that. And there's, you know, talk going, discourse or whatever you call it, going on (MA (Applied) in nursing student).

Confirming what they already knew

A number of the women had commenced university studies with topics that connected with the knowledge they already had from nursing experience. Human development was a frequently mentioned first paper –

Human development was the first one I did, and it actually quite interested me. I suppose because of my nursing training that I'd had, I felt sort of, I mean it was new information but it didn't really challenge me in any way. And it just helped to put a frame around what I was seeing on the job . . . I could make some sort of link between the behaviours I was seeing on the job (hospital trained psychiatric nurse).

This meant that the transition to university study wasn't as difficult as it would have been had they undertaken completely new fields of study. Of surprise to the women was how well they did at their university studies, something they hadn't anticipated –

> Well I started and did several Massey papers, I did human development, individual and social psychology, health studies, introductory anthropology. I started in 1988 and what it did was convince me that I wasn't as dumb as perhaps I had been led to believe. That I could actually do university work (hospital trained psychiatric nurse).

Accessibility of programmes

Other factors that influenced being able to study were the accessibility of the programmes. This accessibility referred to both physical accessibility and other less tangible factors such as approachability of staff.

> I think the timing of the lectures, particularly in the first year, are really hard to get to, because I think that's a crucial year to get you in there and they spread them all over the week. You know and what employer's going to release you for that sort of time. So I find that in particular is bad. I think after you've been there a year you might be able to work around it somehow but you know that crucial first year when you're trying to get your head around it. I mean I had to change my jobs just simply because of that. So that was hard. And I think if there were more user-friendly hours that would be great.

Massey studies were seen as viable options particularly the extramural papers. In a similar way when nursing papers became available at other places like Otago this was mentioned as an impetus for study. When asked what prompted her choice of degree programme and major subject one woman commented –

> Well I suppose because it was available and it was local basically. I didn't have to travel, because I was still working. I still had quite a young family. And so it meant that I could do it here, you know that was the big thing (hospital trained psychiatric nurse, Postgraduate Certificate in Mental Health).

Being available locally was a major factor for a number of women, especially those doing the postgraduate certificates in a clinical area.

Managing home and work and study

For most of the women interviewed the difficulties associated with study were associated with organising their lives rather than the study itself. This finding is reinforced by Blackie.[6] As mentioned earlier, most of the women achieved high standards in their academic work.

> I was dealing with that, dealing with the job change, bringing up two children, totally alone with no childcare support at all, so that was hard. Going to university wasn't hard, I enjoyed the lectures, I enjoyed the study. I don't know what I learnt, I think I've probably just formalised what I knew already.

> And I also enjoyed the intellectual conversation with people – so you know, I enjoyed it, I enjoyed it. But for me the hardest thing was organising all the other stuff going on in my life. And getting there three days a week, the physical getting there was almost harder than doing the assignments and doing the study.

Even working at home often had to be organised around family responsibilities –

> I do my study on my days off, because I was just too tired at night. Some nights I forced myself to, to study. But I also, all through that time I had my father in, he was dying of cancer so that sort of made . . . it would have been easier I think if it wasn't that.

Juggling home and work life was also a factor that influenced when study was undertaken and as the following woman says 'this is my turn now' –

> I've always been a lifelong learner. And with [her husband] studying as intensely as he was and having a new baby, because she was seven months when he started his MBA it wasn't possible for me to really study as well, it was just too difficult. So I just did little things through work really. And so I said to [her husband] I'm putting my life on hold for you really, so that I'm doing the family side of things so you can do what you want to do. I said, 'so when you're finished I'd like it to be my turn.' And so when we came to Wellington it was just, this is my turn now.

Husbands and partners were influential in that if they were supportive the juggling was made much easier:

> The key is a supportive and encouraging husband because if he wasn't fully supportive in wanting me to, you know, to realise myself, then I wouldn't be able to do it. Because he sometimes looks after the children when I've got lectures and so on.

While present husbands may have been supportive, ex-husbands proved to be more negative –

> in fact he told me to do a degree in education and social policy was a total waste of time. If it wasn't a science degree or accounting or business studies – business degree, it wasn't worth the paper it was written on. And as far as he could see it was going to get me nowhere, it was just going to waste four years.

And sometimes it was a matter of proving to husbands and families that their work and study was equally important –

> I managed quite a number of areas and at one point had 100 staff responsible to me . . . But even so of course his job was more important. So in a personal sense I wanted to prove to myself and to him that I could actually achieve this (hospital trained psychiatric nurse, Postgraduate Certificate in Mental Health).

University study as individually enriching

While many of the women spoke about the personal satisfaction of succeeding at university study there were spin-offs in the way that their study influenced others.

> It was good to have the opportunity to sit and talk and discuss things. And also we got various speakers and things in that – people that were probably inaccessible to us otherwise. You know, who were doing great things in mental health. And to hear from them, well it helped me anyway to think there is another way. You know, the way that we do it is not necessarily the way it should be done (hospital trained psychiatric nurse, Postgraduate Certificate in Mental Health).

> But also you get hooked into the reading and the writing and, and I enjoy it. I do like it. And so you know that's why I carry on doing it.

And I like to think that I am setting a good example for my children (hospital trained psychiatric nurse, MA student).

This 'setting a good example for children' was mentioned by many of the women and reflects again the gendered nature of women's work:

I think seeing me there and I think that's been great role modelling and I've never ever discussed a time when not going to university was a possibility (for her sons), so I think they just think well, that's where we have to go.

Gliding up the career pathway

While some of the women interviewed felt their study was necessary for their work situation it was often to maintain their current situation rather than to gain advancement. It seems that credentialing is a factor in all workplaces and advanced qualifications are deemed essential to keep up with the pace of change in the health work force. In the following account a woman who has 25 years clinical experience talks about her concern about her own qualifications becoming redundant when compared with graduates emerging with degrees. Her situation as a sole mother made her situation seem even more acute to her.

During that time our marriage broke up. So I really needed to, I'd got to like a crisis I guess where I knew that I needed to increase my income. I didn't know how I would do it around the kids and I think that's when I decided that I could use the little bit of maintenance money and if I did agency work, I could probably go to varsity and get a degree because at that time there was all this talk about career pathways coming in and lots of pressure to do something. *And I could see that the new nurses coming out were all going to go gliding up the career pathway with their new degrees and what was going to happen to all the hospital nurses.* And I could see this system of stratification sort of coming before my eyes and I thought well I couldn't even guarantee I'll have a job if I don't go to varsity (hospital trained general nurse, Cardiothoracic Nursing Certificate, BA).

This nurse's experience is mirrored by others. While she undertook her degree with the hope that she would end up in a more secure and better paid position she is now employed in nursing work that is paying her less than she received when she was agency nursing. This she finds ironic, as it was her study in social policy for her degree that was stated as giving her the edge at her recent interview –

[The new employer] totally disregarded my degree and yet they told me at the interview that the reason they would like to offer me the job was because I had the degree. And that I would be involved in policy making, education and nursing and they thought it was a perfect degree to help my nursing. And it actually has already been useful, and they're already asking me a lot, for a lot of advice that they wouldn't be able to get if I hadn't done that degree. So I'm already feeding into the system and yet they offered me thirty-five thousand to start with.

However, the possibility of a career pathway and the job satisfaction that she is obtaining in this new area has made it possible to accept low monetary rewards initially.

I think there is a much better career pathways structure than there is in, say, practice nursing.

This is not something she is prepared to tolerate long term, which she recognises as a dilemma –

Ah, so I have that dilemma at the moment you know, like here's a job that I really love, here's a job with potential that I could get passionate about. That has lots of places that you could go from but . . . but I can't see it keeping me happy long term unless they come up with some salary rise.

This perception that all nurses are now better qualified is also echoed in the following account –

Well, I guess again I was enjoying my job and I thought well, you know, I've done quite OK in the comprehensive training, why don't I push myself on a wee bit further, see if I can do something a bit more. *Because everybody else seemed to be doing something extra.* And I thought well OK I'll give it a go (enrolled nurse, registered comprehensive nurse).

Further education for nurses increases career options and choices. Lumby[7] articulates this well when she states –

professional women today, particularly university educated ones, are less likely to put up with poor working conditions and lack of recognition of their expertise and their level of responsibility. The nurses I have interviewed who have moved careers spoke to me of now being openly valued for their contribution to their workplace, of being less stressed and of having improved work conditions.

This is a key issue of contention for the health service sector to address if they wish to retain experienced nurses.

The future

These women were pursuing study that was flexible but that also stretched them intellectually. There is a tension between providing a supportive environment and ensuring that intellectual boundaries are pushed.

> I keep feeling that I don't have the skills that I feel I should have at this stage of my study. I don't know a lot about research methods and although I'm going to be doing a research project this year I still don't feel I have a lot of knowledge about the whole thing. And I think that, I mean someone said in our first class that, you know, we're going to found out for the frauds that we are. Well that is exactly how I feel . . . I mean I can write better than I ever used to, I have a better picture of the bigger environment, mental health services and so on. Because now I read an awful lot and I keep up to date as much as I can, but I just feel in terms of, the sort of, some of the particular research skills, I wish there was more.

This quote illustrates what can be gained by university study but it also highlights the raised expectations that go along with this experience.

This chapter focuses on the experiences of a specific cohort of women. Some of their experiences, such as the hospital training system, are unique to this group of women. Despite this difference, however, there are many similarities between these women and the women who are currently entering nursing as a career. The similarities pertain to the gendered nature of the occupation and of the wider society. Most women, regardless of career paths taken, go on to have the main responsibility for children that they bear and this impacts on their participation in the labour market and also on how and when they engage in further education.

Postscript – the authors and nursing

As the authors of this chapter we also mirror many of the characteristics of the respondents to this study. We both completed our nursing training in hospital schools of nursing in 1970 (Alison Dixon at Lower Hutt and Allison Kirkman at Christchurch) and both registered as general and obstetric nurses.[8] Both of us have worked in a variety of clinic settings (Alison Dixon in theatre, surgery, intensive care and staff development and Allison Kirkman in coronary care, intensive care and neonatal intensive care). Our point of difference has been our academic pathway.

Alison Dixon became a full-time university student soon after registration and worked part-time in practice in her university holidays around family responsibilities. Nursing was not available as an academic discipline at that time and her BA is in psychology and anthropology. Her subsequent Diploma in Social Sciences and PhD were in nursing and reflected the common pattern of the women participants in that this study was undertaken while juggling family and full-time work commitments in nursing. Alison Dixon is the head of a school of nursing that offers both undergraduate and postgraduate nursing education and specialises in professional issues as they affect nurses and nursing.

After her initial practice experiences Allison Kirkman completed her midwifery registration in Christchurch and did her first university paper (psychology 101) as part of her Diploma in Nursing at the School of Advanced Nursing Studies. Her BA was then completed extramurally through Massey University while she worked first as a tutor in a hospital school of nursing and then in a polytechnic school of nursing. However, her BA, BA (Hons) and later PhD were in sociology and she now works as a senior lecturer in sociology and specialises in gender, sexuality and health including the study of nurses and nursing work.

Notes

1 Nursing Council of New Zealand (2001).
2 Anne Witz (1994) p.23.
3 While all the women in this chapter have obtained further educational qualifications than their initial nursing registration we have stated this initial registration after each direct quotation to indicate the commencement of career pathways. Where it is relevant to the quotation we also indicate the university programme undertaken.
4 Middleton (1987) p.79.

5   Doyal (1995) p.169.
6   Blackie (2001).
7   Lumby (2001) p.30.
8   Abbreviations for nursing and midwifery qualifications used in this chapter are those recognised by the Nursing Council of New Zealand. The registrations referred to in this chapter are:

Registered Comprehensive Nurse	RCpN
Registered General and Obstetric Nurse	RGON
Registered Psychiatric Nurse	RPN
Registered Midwife	RM
Enrolled Nurse	EN

In addition to these the Nursing Council recognises three other qualifications: Registered General Nurse (RGN), Registered Obstetric Nurse (RON) and Registered Psychopaedic Nurse (RPdN). From 2001 there will be the opportunity for nurses who qualify as expert clinicians to apply for the title of Nurse Practitioner. If awarded this will be stated on the Annual Practicing Certificate along with their scope of practice, for example, family health, adult health, child health, women's health, health of the elderly, occupational health and mental health.

7

'AGEPROOFING' YOUR CAREER – AGE, GENDER AND THE 'NEW CAREER'

Deborah Jones and Sarah Proctor-Thomson

Third age careers?

Midlife management education is a collision site for conflicting stories about ageing and career. In the postindustrial west of the 21st century, 50 is supposed to be the new 40, 40 the new 30, middle age to be the beginning of a second and productive adulthood, a 'third age career'.[1] In the rhetoric of the 'new career', we will have many different jobs and professional roles during our lifetimes, and it is up to us to constantly reinvent ourselves.[2] But in the lifetimes of those who are now middle-aged and older, not only have seniority systems been overthrown astonishingly fast, being older is a positive disadvantage for most, and the later stages of working life are haunted by the spectres of redundancy, unemployment and underemployment.[3] From this point of view, the age scales have slid down, rather than up – at 40, or even 30, job seekers are seen as 'too old'.[4] Perhaps 30 is the new 50? Particularly puzzling for many commentators, this disadvantage seems to be intensifying, rather than dissolving, despite demographics showing that the workforce will continue to age into the 21st century as the baby boomers work their way through.[5]

Add to this picture the complexities of gender and career for a cohort of women who were brought up in the 1950s and earlier, when most women were not expected to have careers at all. We interviewed older women who were engaged in midlife management education. Although the workforce they entered as adults systematically disadvantages women, most were already successful as managers, even senior managers. We might imagine that they would clearly be among those fortunate ones for whom skills, experience and connections would ensure confidence and the security of well-paid employment. As we will show, even these privileged women bought into the idea that once a person is past a certain age, there is somehow an inevitable decline in competency. They embodied the conflicting stories of limitation and also possibility involved in ageing, gender and career. In looking specifically at how midlife education fits into this framework, we argue that management education offers the promise of 'ageproofing' – of compensating for the perceived decrease in workplace competence that comes with middle age.[6]

Over the hill? Introducing the study

Like gender, age identity is a relational pattern in which we are all implicated. But it is accepted that we move through age categories over a lifetime. As Kirkwood has put it, 'it is not "them and us" we are dealing with, but "us and us".'[7] As a 'younger' and an 'older' researcher, we became increasingly sensitised to how age and perceptions of age shaped the research process. We adopted the term 'older' from the 'Education in Mid and Later Life' research project, where it is defined as 40 and over. When we applied for ethics approval, we were advised not to use the term 'older' on the information sheet, because this could imply to participants that they were 'over the hill'. This alerted us to the way that a simple reference to relative age could point to a painful topic, frequently dealt with by euphemism, omission, or 'passing'. This phenomenon recurred during the interview process. Interviews were carried out by Sarah, our 'younger' researcher. She found – to her surprise – that she responded with discomfort to asking the question: 'How do you see yourself as an older woman manager?' Participants often responded with embarrassed laughter, blank stares or indignant responses such as, 'oh thank you very much!'. These responses highlighted the discomforts and complexities of being an 'older' woman in the workplace as they played out in the interviews. We remembered that it is still considered normal for 'women of a certain age' to lie about or at least conceal their ages.

Our broad research question is: How do older women managers see management education in the context of their careers? This question addresses a number of related issues: the position of older workers (managers in this case); the 'new career' context for managers; and the position of women managers two decades on from the first wave of equal employment opportunity policies. The core of our work is a 'de-naturalising critique', in the words of feminist rhetorician Judith Butler.[8] Using a feminist discourse analysis, we set out to question the boundaries of age and gender rather than to take them as given – to consider how 'age' and 'gender' are constructed in the management context, and to consider the effects of these constructions for women's lives.[9] In common with other contributors to this book, we have used a life-history approach in designing our interview schedule and reading the interview texts – that is, we asked women about their whole life and career stories, as well as more specific questions about their careers now and their experiences of management education. This method takes a longitudinal perspective that provides rich data on careers within the fullness of individual's lives, while simultaneously positioning these accounts within broader social and professional trends.[10] To put the interviews in context we used published data on older women in the New Zealand workforce as well as academic and popular cultural texts on gender, ageing and career. We also reflected on our own experiences of age and gender, during and beyond the research process. In this chapter we will cite both academic and popular sources to show the range of texts we drew on.

From the 'Education in Mid and Later Life' survey we drew a sample of 20 women who were majoring in management at Victoria University and were willing to be interviewed. Of this group 18 women were currently, or had previously been, in a management role, and the same number were involved in full-time work while studying part-time. Our participants were aged between 41 and 55. We drew on the data provided from the postal survey to ensure that the broadest possible range of occupations, marital status and educational backgrounds of older management students was represented. All the women were Pākehā except for one ethnic Indian. This homogeneity is important, because our taken-for-granted values about ageing (as well as gender and career) vary from one cultural context to another.

Compared to other women in the 'Education in Mid and Later Life' survey, the women in our sample, as a group, were more likely to work full-time, to be sponsored by their employers and to indicate that work demands were the main barriers to study. They had higher incomes; were less likely to report difficulties in studying; and more likely to cite new knowledge and qualifications as their main motivation to study.

Our semi-structured interviews began with the women's early aspirations and worked up to the present, focussing around these central questions:

- How do older women managers see their careers now?
- How have their ideas about careers changed during their lives?
- How do they see themselves and others as 'older women managers', and how do they think they are seen by others?
- How do they see management education in the context of their careers?

After preliminary analysis we held a feedback session which was attended by about a third of participants. We taped and transcribed the discussion, which we fed into our analysis.

The value of claims we make here, based on interviews with this small sample, depends on how persuasively we make sense of them within their social context. In looking for patterns and inconsistencies in the interview accounts, we see them in terms of social patterns, not individual coherence or inconsistency.[11]

'I can't put it down to sexism any longer' – the gendering of age and the ageing of gender

> Just when you get white hair people treat you differently. They assume you're a bit doddery, that you're not quite up with the play. That I don't know, yeah I'm becoming more and more conscious of it. I'm not saying that I notice it all the time but there are, there are times when I'm sort of, say, ignored in a conversation and I'll realise that 'no I can't put it down to sexism any longer. You know it's because I'm old' (Evelyn).[12]

Older women managers do not come naively to the experience of age discrimination. Most have encountered gender discrimination in what is even now a non-traditional occupation for women.[13] In the comment above, Evelyn covers several key issues that recur in our analysis: the relationship between gender and age; perceptions of competence; and the body as the index of age. In this section we will discuss what women said about these issues. The focal area of interest in our analysis is the interaction of discourses of ageing, gender, and careers. Integral to this analysis is the understanding that none of these work independently of the others. For example, 'ageing' has differing implications for different genders, and varies in significance in relation to stage of career. The concept of 'competence' is an important nexus in our discussion, because competence – and perceived competence – is associated with the ways that people are evaluated in terms of age and gender in the workplace. Competence links to career prospects and to education as a way to enhance competencies and thus career prospects – hence 'employability'.

We begin by considering how 'older women managers' are seen and evaluated. The answers to these questions depended on whether we asked participants to talk about others or about themselves, or in terms of how they thought that others saw them. When we asked them to talk about the general image of older women managers, most participants evoked a positive picture. Grace suggested that the current image of older women managers was as –

> Pretty effective actually, I think there's some very, I mean looking around in New Zealand at the moment you have to say the role models are pretty strong. Some of them are high profile some are lesser profile, yeah. No I think they've got a good image, effective (Grace).

Participants noted experience and confidence, and the idea that older women managers have earned their position and are therefore deserving.

> I suspect having a view and or an opinion and not being reticent in putting it forward might be one of those descriptives. A sense of when I think of me and my peers, a sense of having worked to get where you are and therefore it matters. Rather than it not necessarily [being] your birthright, it's your right because you've earned it and worked [for] it (Helen).

However, they were much less positive when they were asked to look though the eyes of others. Like Evelyn who thought that others discounted her as 'a bit doddery . . . not quite up with the play', other women saw young people as 'judging you on age' (Mary). They also saw themselves as more disadvantaged by age than their male peers: 'some staff below you won't see you as being an authority figure in a way that they would see a man in your age group' (Kristin). This perception is validated by recent local research with workers and employers which highlights a double jeopardy for older women, who were judged more harshly as they aged. About 18.6% of respondents felt that performance declined in men by 54 years, but 31.3% believed this to be so for women. This finding echoes similar findings in other western workforces.[14]

It is not surprising then that most participants sought to distance themselves from the label of being 'older'. Despite the previous positive responses about the image of older women managers, when we asked explicitly about how they saw *themselves* as older women managers, the picture was slightly inconsistent. Only three of the 20 women were comfortable with the label of 'older women manager'. While two women felt that they were not yet adequately experienced and skilled to deserve the label, the majority did not want to be associated with the negative traits of being 'older'. For example, despite her previous accolade to 'older women managers', Grace did not want to put herself in the same category: 'I mean I don't think I behave like an older woman. I don't think much like an older woman but of course I am one, and I probably do, I just don't think I do.' When Grace was asked how older women behave, she accused the interviewer of cornering her –

> Oh well, that's a trick question, yeah well they don't behave any way do they because they're as different as chalk from cheese and there's plenty of younger women who behave like older women and some older women who behave like real brats. (Grace)

Responses such as this highlight the contradictions in the identity of an 'older women manager'. There is a dislocation between abstract perceptions of age, and incorporation of the concept of 'older' as part of one's own identity: 'It's the difference between accepting the category [of older women managers] and accepting yourself as part of it (laughing). (Melanie)

This tendency to divorce oneself from such a demographic group appears to arise from the widely held belief that ageing is synonymous with reduced capabilities and decreasing competency. Again, despite the previous positive attributions Helen ascribed to older women managers, she later suggested that because she is still competent she is not old: ' I mean I don't think of myself as being older, I mean I see all the evidence that I'm older than I used to be, but I don't feel that my age impacts on my ability to do my work' (Helen). The quote suggests that if you remain competent and maintain a high level of performance, then you do not have to wear the label of 'older'. In other words 'competence' counteracts the otherwise negative images of ageing. Many comments made by the participants emphasised the division between chronological age and work-based competence: '[Competence] depends on my work ethic, my skills, that's how it's judged, it's not judged according to my age' (Greta). And in Mary's words –

> For women to succeed in [management] roles you just have to be seen as an equal on a career footing regardless of your gender or your age whether you've got grey hair or whatever . . . So for [older] women managers, they need to be seen as just as capable of doing the job.

Therefore, the classification of 'older' or 'old' is argued to be invalid in assessing competence, or as a basis for perceptions of performance and potential. These beliefs echo typical equal opportunity discourse that argues for treatment of individuals based on their work skills and merit. But as feminist critics have pointed out, the quest for an 'objective' standard of merit can only ever have limited purchase in an environment where the standard male (young, white) template is the arbiter of merit and so of competence (Burton, 1992).

The implicit bias in various formulations of merit showed up when we asked what women meant when they spoke of 'competence'. In this context, competence included characteristics such as 'youthful attitude', 'young at heart' and 'willingness to learn new things'. For example –

> I think older women, that I've worked with anyway, that have had responsible jobs, if they keep an open mind and they keep young at heart in learning new things and stuff like that, you know they're quite good to work with (Patricia).

In contrast with positive terms such as 'experienced', 'skilled', and 'confident', used in the earlier sections of the interviews to describe older workers, here women are seen as competent as long as they maintain a kind of inner youth –

> So I have to think about myself as an older woman manager, as long as I keep young I guess that's alright. I don't want to be an old type manager because with that comes the stigma of old ideas and not relearning and those sorts of things. As long as I keep myself young in my knowledge, I think that's the most important thing. But I don't have any real hang-ups about that [being an older women manager] at all. (Katherine)

Youthful competence is strongly associated with learning, a 'youthful, still-want-to-learn sort of attitude' (Patricia), and in essence older women are keeping themselves young by continuously learning: 'For women managers, if they want to remain in management roles, key to them remaining effective is to be a lifelong learner, to keep on learning' (Beverley).

These responses suggest that in order to combat ageing, one simply needs to be perceived as younger, or at least youthful. However, where competence and learning are linked to being 'young', the epithet 'old' is reinforced as a mark of incompetence, which can only be deferred or masked. Many of our participants wanted to manage age at work by separating the mind and psychological attitudes – 'competence' or 'work ethic' – from the gendered or ageing body. Like gender, age as an identity category is typically naturalised, so that our ideas about how competent you can be are referred back to a set of assumptions about biology and the body. This then puts our assumptions about age or gender beyond challenge or change. Associated with biological naturalisation is a set of psychological discourses about what is natural and appropriate from a developmental point of view at a given age or for a woman or a man. Thus certain prescribed age and gender attitudes and abilities are normalised.

The relationship between the body, age and competence is spelled out in the efforts that women make to manage their body image at work.

I am quite conscious of image . . . I usually try to look the part . . . Like, I would never risk coming to work looking sort of frumpy or shabby in the way I dress, where I think a man can risk that a lot more readily without his image being undermined (Kristin).

The techniques our participants used to 'look the part' were typically methods of appearing younger, healthier and more vital. It seems that competence through the right attitude and a 'willingness to learn' described above, may also require a more overt and tangible display of youthfulness. Some of the participants used their fitness as evidence that they were not old, but rather valuable and competent –

I run marathons, not every week, but I do. I do a whole raft of things, I still want to learn, I still want to do new things, I still want to contribute and hope to be able to do that for some time. (Helen)

The display of fitness in the workplace is an important aspect of the appearance of competence, especially for women.[15] Although the women we spoke to were aware of the normalised forms of competence and did not wish to conform to these norms, precisely because they *were* controls, they were in fact unable to resist –

> You want those judgements to be made on your ability to do your career, not what you look like. So just as you know I colour my hair because I've got some grey hair, my mother had grey hair, it's got, as far as I'm concerned, absolutely nothing to do with age. It's all about genetics. But I know that in the place that I work, grey-haired women are not seen as success material so you colour your hair and I always used to say no way am I going to dye my hair just to satisfy someone else's image problem but nevertheless you do it because you want to keep your job. (Mary)

Here the imagined gaze of the other is a controlling device which is internalised more or less reluctantly, and to a greater or lesser extent.[16]

'Identity management' thus becomes increasingly important in 'an uncertain world [which] contains elements that are simultaneously threatening and encouraging to experiments with identity in later life'.[17] Frequently there is a separation of the 'old' body from the 'real' person within. This split is emphasised where age and competency are seen as antithetical. While our participants could see that many [chronologically] older women were highly competent, and could even name some advantages to being older, at the same time they tended to code 'competent' as 'youthful'. Rather than actually contesting the idea that age brings decline, they tried to manage the stigma of increasing age by both passing as young as much as possible and by maintaining an inner sense of a 'youthful' self. In effect they reinforced the equation of age with incompetence by not 'really' being, or appearing to be, old. Their involvement in management education was both an inner reassurance that they were youthful mentally and psychologically, and a kind of external badge of youthful competency in a workforce that is not friendly to older workers.

Wiping out on the knowledge wave over 40

> Try surfing the much touted knowledge wave if you are much over 40 and chances are you'll wipe out . . . yet captains of industry loudly

fret about brain drain, lack of management nous, and skills shortages (New Zealand newspaper article[18]).

Our study is located within current anxieties about age and work, exemplified by articles like the one above, printed in the popular press and in the popular management literature. Like the one cited here, such articles typically contrast the demographics of the ageing baby boomers with 'irrational' and 'illogical' prejudices against older workers. Among evidence of age discrimination, the unique qualities of older workers – e.g., 'the ability to sift fads from real changes' – are promoted, side by side with recommendations to older workers to make themselves look youthful:

> Resumes . . . should convey vitality through listing leisure pursuits such as playing squash and progressive thinking: 'Currently studying Java programming'.[19]

Like the accounts given by our research participants, such articles indicate the conflicting contemporary discourse of ageing. Although commentators may point out how irrational age discrimination is – that 'smart businesses' will draw on older workers and avoid the 'scrap heap mentality' which damages business, not to mention possible legal action for discrimination;[20] that the 'millennium time bomb'[21] of demographic change is inevitable, and that employers must adjust – it seems that like sexism and racism at work, age discrimination is a cultural phenomenon that goes beyond the simple common sense of human resources 'best practice' and the 'business case' for change.

The rapid rise in the consideration of ageing parallels the fast approaching and inevitable entry of the baby boomers into the status of 'senior citizens'. The economic impact of this group leaving paid work and becoming reliant on governmental systems has driven a major push for investigation and research into the area of older workers. Government policy has moved to promote the positive aspects of prolonged work lives, and hopeful estimates suggest people will stay in paid work for many more years than previous cohorts.[22] In fact older people are not only 'allowed' but in fact required to work longer for economic reasons as the horizon of pension eligibility recedes, and increased savings are required to cover more of the expenses of old age. Ironically, at the same time as this major push for people to stay in the workforce longer, there has been an equally influential and rapid dissolution of traditional hierarchies that were based on age and tenure. Thus, in a time when managers in their 20s and 30s, valued for their energy, youth, and contemporary knowledge, are placed in primary positions of responsibility and control, older workers are also being encouraged to continue in paid work. These movements have come into conflict with one another.

A mounting body of literature identifies pervasive negative perceptions of older workers, while at the same time rates of job loss have risen for this group. In addition, it seems that older women in particular are susceptible to biases against older workers, i.e. they are seen as less competent at earlier ages.[23] Ageing is particularly a feminist issue because women typically live longer than men, yet have less opportunity to develop careers and economic resources.[24]

There is still very little research on older women's career patterns.[25] The women we interviewed are part of a cohort who entered the work force in greater numbers than ever before on the back of the second wave of feminism. Most did not grow up planning a 'career' and as managers most have encountered discrimination or at least minority status in what is even now a non-traditional occupation for women.[26] It is ironic that just as they are entering seniority in their field, seniority itself is becoming a basis of disadvantage. Feminists may suspect a plot against women. We see the current situation as the effects of a number of converging changes. Against the claims of the 'new career' literature – that lifelong learning and constant career change provide the template for employability – we argue that the new discourses of age and competence dis-able all but the few from 'mid-career' onwards.

During the last two decades, intergenerational disparities in power have shifted. The political economy in Aotearoa/New Zealand, as elsewhere in the west, has shifted to accentuate the sovereignty of the individual who is assumed to be responsible for creating their own life circumstances.[27] A series of restructurings in the public and private sector have made swathes of older workers redundant, and many of those who still have work have been marginalised into a casualised workforce. Cheaper younger workers have been privileged in both employment and promotion. Along with these changes, dominant career paradigms – which were once discussed and debated specifically in terms of movement within organisational systems and structures – have given way to models of the 'new career' which extends beyond organisational, occupational, industrial and national boundaries.[28] These new forms of career are based on the idea of the individual as a free and active agent in career development and progression. Individual skills, ability, and competence have become the tools of the careerist, tools that can be transferred from one location to the next, and are available for trade or purchase. The entrepreneurial self is constantly in the process of producing 'brand me'.[29]

The 'new careers' or 'boundaryless career' literature argues that this career model frees individual actors from the constraints of organisational systems, and empowers them to develop and build their careers as they will, opening up the opportunities to move through multiple careers over the course of a lifetime. But, more recently, feminist career theorists have pointed out that many groups in the population will not have, or be able to develop, the marketable and saleable skills necessary to make this model work for them, even in the affluent west.[30] For the privileged ones who can, the price tends to be a massive commitment to long hours and high energy – another factor which tends to favour younger workers. Coded adjectives for youth, such as 'energy' and 'passion', are ubiquitous in job advertisements. Not only does the 'new career' narrative present an incomplete picture which excludes much of the workforce, it has the effect of blaming individuals for their lack of career success by normalising the proposition that as far as work is concerned 'your destiny is in your own hands'.[31] By extension, individuals are blamed for their lack of economic and social success.

During our feedback session participants indicated that they had taken on this doctrine of individual responsibility and incorporated it in their accounts of their life and career choices, and their commitment to study was seen as an extension of it. Mary described herself after completion of her degree as –

> Like the rest of you I think, trying to pick up the house and the garden and redecorating and catch up with the family because they've all been ignored but I also feel a little lost because I think I've sort of sunk back to the, [to] not being disciplined.

This self-discipline discourse was also applied retrospectively to the entire life history. Katherine explains that the interview process for our study had triggered a reframing of her career –

I'm basically lazy, I think I was bright enough to do what was needed but didn't do much work at school and my brother had gone, who was older than me, had gone off to university and done things . . . he'd done a PhD and it wasn't regarded as particularly necessary for me. I came from a farming background [and] I wanted to go farming, wasn't allowed because it wasn't a woman thing to do and my father really couldn't see that that would have been appropriate at all for any woman to be on a farm and that's how it was then, which was sort of late 60s early 70s and that sort of thing just didn't happen very often. But the interview, as I said, it just really made me think about it and made me quite embarrassed that I had really been quite so lazy and, and perhaps disinterested in any study at all.

In her comments, Katherine recognises the powerful societal constraints on her life and career choices ('it wasn't a women thing to do') but ultimately blames herself for her failure to achieve more in her life ('I'm basically lazy'). It is paradoxical that our questions triggered this account, because as researchers our feminist account would have been very different, positioning Katherine as disempowered by patriarchal attitudes. Similarly, we initially looked for the 'Educating Rita' type of narrative in our interview accounts, the narrative in which older women are empowered by midlife education and given a second chance to break away from the constraining sexism of their upbringings. However, times have changed. For our participants, as for many others in the workforce, education has been not so much emancipatory as instrumental.[32]

It seems clear from our analysis of the available statistical data that education advantages women in the workforce. But while women are becoming increasingly more qualified, they lag behind their male counterparts in both salaries and employment rates. Data suggests that, generally, tertiary education benefits men financially more than it does women. Women are also less likely to be employed than men at all levels of educational attainment. The difference between the employment rates of men and women becomes larger as the level of qualification decreases.[33] In order to receive greater financial recognition it is more important for women to distinguish themselves from the rest of the pack through academic credentials than it is for men.

Management education as ageproofing

> If you want to ageproof yourself, you have to think about how you're
> coming across to people. You have to think about the way you dress,
> your hair, your whole persona. You've got to look contemporary . . .
> make sure you have a laptop on your desk. Get an electronic organiser.
> (Advice given by a popular management magazine.)[34]

Throughout his chapter we have distinguished various versions of 'age-proofing', from rewriting the body to seem youthful, erasing signs of age and displaying signs of fitness; to accessorising with electronic equipment and related accomplishments such as Java programming (most unlikely to be of value in any job but programming); to learning itself as the index of eternal career change, employability and creating one's own destiny.

The emphasis on lifelong learning among our participants may not be surprising, given that our sampling frame was people involved in midlife education. Their descriptions of their reasons for study and their experiences of education are much as we might expect from their characteristics outlined earlier. However, their comments are echoed in the literature, both popular and academic. Most women did not report the breakthroughs in understanding or major new insights such as we might find in an emancipatory narrative: rather, the learning experience was in line with the ideas and experiences they encountered at work and provided validation rather than novelty.

> What I wanted from the studying was either knowledge that what I
> was doing was right, you know the way I managed or the how I
> managed. Or if I was doing it wrong then I was going to get the
> knowledge of how to do it right. So I think it was really used as an
> extension of what I was doing . . . The reinforcement that the path
> I'm taking is the correct path. (Ria)

As well as personal validation, the degree offered legitimation and advantage in the eyes of others –

> I wanted a credential. I wanted something that was recognisable,
> something that gave me credibility. I wanted something that was
> going to set me aside or apart from anybody else. (Ellen)

Many women also found that what they were learning was of practical value: 'at times I'd be coming straight out of a lecture and into a situation where I'd be putting that knowledge into practice straightaway, even on the same day'. (Beverley) She also looked for 'conceptual depth to the knowledge of management'.

While not all the women were able to make the career moves they hoped for directly after completing their qualifications, others got new jobs or promotions soon after. Either way, most reported in interviews that they were satisfied with their experience. However, one woman who was new to university expressed disappointment that there was little of the debate and stimulation that she hoped for. In the feedback session too, most women expressed tension between their professional expertise and their position as students, often feeling sceptical about what their teachers, as academics, had to offer them as practitioners, and critical about that they saw as lapses of professionalism on the part of their teachers.

One woman summed up a number of the key issues when asked if she was studying to actually learn or mainly for the qualification –

I think it's both actually.

1   I think there are things I need to know for work. I think it will help me, the particular papers I've chosen . . . will give me some *technical skills* that I don't have sufficiently now so that will actually help me directly in my work.

2   Also having those it does *add to my credibility* in the workplace and *my status* in the workplace and it will help *my promotion chances* in future, there's no doubt about that.

3   But the other aspect that's really important is it also *helps my confidence.* Confidence is related to how you actually perform, you know you sort of perform to the level that you expect yourself to perform at.

4   But it's partly the credentialism thing where the importance of the qualifications is the fact that you've got the qualifications – you know what I mean? It says something about you the fact that *you've been able to go away and get the qualifications* rather than anything specific that those qualifications help you with in terms of the content of your work. (Kristin) (emphasis and numbering added).

In this account it is not only useful to know technical things but to be seen as knowledgeable and to be seen as the kind of person who gets qualifications.

Critical writers on management education have long argued that it fails to open up the vital questions facing people in organisations. Its pedagogy reduces these questions to technicalities or papers over them with buzzwords. Feminists have also criticised the way that most management education ignores the complexities of women manager's lives.[35] Management education in a sense sells itself as a solution, rather than equipping students with critical tools to examine their own situation. In this respect we believe that management education can be distinguished from other professionally oriented midlife programmes in areas such as nursing and teaching, where critical and reflexive perspectives are more integrated. Dyer and Humphries argue that '[Students] seem prepared to shape themselves in ways purported to meet the anticipated values and needs of future organisations. Less evident is their willingness or ability to challenge this future as one that is neither necessary or inevitable.'[36] We could also argue, as advocates, that the women we talked with were so used to marginalising and discounting, or even hiding, the attributes of gender and age at work, that they are unlikely to engage with these issues as an aspect of their management education, especially in the presence of male peers.

Our analysis of the interviews brings out the social contradictions that they embody. We have also argued that that competence is not some stand-alone neutral attribute, but rather that *various* perceptions of competence are what make the difference. Unlike some of the women we talked with, we do not consider that problems such as ageism can be solved by splitting away identity categories such as age or gender so that 'personhood of the person is still intact' as Judith Butler puts it.[37]

One version of such an attempt is expressed here by Jane –

> I sort of see people as people, and I see their personality rather than their age. I tend to find age is rather irrelevant unless I'm trying to find an explanation as to why they're doing something. Sometimes age is relevant then because it might be you know people of a certain age I suppose have been brought up with certain ideas and that might affect their behaviour so generally I see individual people not related to their age.

Jane likes to 'see people as people' and tries not to include age in this perception . . . that is except if age becomes relevant. How and why it can become relevant to competence, and who decides when and how it is relevant, are the critical issues. Jane may have little control over how and why others may perceive her as older or female.

The gendered quality of both age and managerial careers means that the negotiation of being 'older' + 'woman' + 'manager' is particularly fraught with the danger of being seen as incompetent, de-skilled, 'not success material'. The struggle to retain the impression of competence involved, for the women we talked with, a reframing of 'youth' and 'age' in which age is disguised or deferred rather than destigmatised. The ageing body is decoupled from the still-'youthful' and therefore competent mind, heart and 'attitude'. Management education plays an important part in this process as a sign of lifelong learning, technical competence and the energy of ambition. It offers continuous learning, flexibility, and adaptability as qualifications in themselves, but ignores the argument that they are only possible for a select group of people that have the resources, the time and the appropriate types of responsibilities that allow for midlife education. As we have seen, even for a select group such as the women we interviewed, education can offer 'ageproofing' to only a limited extent. The act of denying the 'negative' aspects of age does nothing to deconstruct negative stereotypes about 'older' women, it just suppresses them or defers them to a later 'biological' stage. As Molly Andrews points out eloquently: 'denial of difference . . . strips the old of their history and leaves them with nothing to offer but a mimicry of their youth'.[38]

The idea that careers are now 'boundaryless' – that we can have multiple careers throughout our lifetimes and that lifelong learning can ageproof us – is radically challenged by the experience and perceptions of women ageing in the workforce, and by the research that presents patterns of ageism in employment and in unemployment. Midlife management education offers women some 'competitive advantage' in relation to men and over other women. But it does little to challenge the gradual devaluing that even these accomplished and privileged women are facing as they age, and that may be equally or even more powerful in determining their future careers.

Notes

1   Curnow, Fox, & Blass (1994).
2   Arthur & Rousseau (1996), Arthur, Inkson, & Pringle (1999).
3   McGregor p.201; McGregor & Grey (2001).

4   Ibid, Doward & Rigby (2000).
5   Henderson (2002), Sparrow (1999), White (1999).
6   Doward & Rigby (2000).
7   Kirkwood (2001).
8   Butler (1990).
9   We take 'discourse' to include: Ways of constituting knowledge – what is true? and who says so?; The social practices – what we do as well as what we say; Forms of subjectivity – who are we? in which situations? who says so?; Power relations – what are the strategic effects of these knowledges, subjectivities & practices?; And the relations between them – how do these all interact over time & in particular locations? (Weedon (1987)).
10 Middleton (1993).
11 Garnsey & Rees (1996).
12 All participants are identified by a pseudonym throughout the following discussion.
13 McGregor, Thomson & Dewe (1994), National Advisory Council (1994).
14 McGregor (2001).
15 Tretheway (1999).
16 Linstead & Grafton-Small (1992).
17 Biggs (1997) p.553.
18 Henderson (2002).
19 Ibid.
20 Lucas (2000), Sparrow (1999), Steinhauser (1998), White (1999).
21 Stuller (2000).
22 Thomson (2001).
23 McGregor (1999), McGregor and Grey (2001).
24 Browne (1998).
25 Still & Timms (1998).
26 McGregor, Thomson & Dewe (1994), National Advisory Council (1994).
27 Biggs (1997).
28 Arthur, Inkson & Pringle (1999).
29 Peters (1999).
30 Pringle & Mallon (2001).
31 Moses (2001).
32 Benn, Elliott, & Whaley (1998).
33 Statistics New Zealand (1996).
34 Doward (2000).
35 Mavin & Bryans (1999), Dehler, Welsh, & Lewis (2001).
36 Dyer & Humphries (1999) p.2.
37 Butler, p.61.
38 Andrews (1999) p.316s.

8

REDUNDANCY AS AN OPPORTUNITY – JOB LOSS AND EDUCATION IN MIDLIFE

Judith A Davey

Redundancy and its meanings

Wide-ranging technological, economic and political changes in recent years have had a destabilising impact on labour markets throughout the world. The result has been greater flexibility in work processes and locations, but also unemployment, redundancy and more volatile careers. Concern is widely expressed about older people who lose their jobs and who may experience difficulty in re-entering paid work. In this chapter the focus is on the experience of redundancy in midlife and how it may lead to educational participation, rather than on the reasons why redundancy or other changes in the labour market occur.

In a dictionary definition, anything which is redundant is surplus to requirements. In industrial relations terms a worker who is redundant is one whose job position is no longer in existence, for example when an enterprise or part of an organisation closes or is restructured. Redundancy can also be specific to an individual and can happen at any level of staffing, within any sector of the workforce and to workers of any age. Some of the respondents in the 'Education in Mid and Later Life' survey experienced redundancy in the formal and legal sense. However, redundancy was self-defined in the responses. People were able to extend the definition of redundancy to include being forced out of a job for personal and organisational reasons which might not have stood up to legal scrutiny.

The 'redundancy' group

Out of the total 959 postal survey respondents, 14% suggested that redundancy or job loss (affecting themselves or their spouse) had been a trigger for involvement in education at Victoria University. Compared to total respondents, a higher proportion of this group were male (37%, total 29%) and a higher proportion were studying full-time (41%, total 24%). They were represented at all levels of study, but a high proportion were taking either undergraduate degrees or vocational qualifications/ subjects (for example, in education, law, library and information studies, nursing and midwifery, or public policy). The motivations for study among the 'redundancy' group were more frequently job related than for the older students as a whole and a higher proportion were out of the workforce when they began their current studies (26%, total 16%). The redundancy group were spread over the socio-economic groups, but contained a higher proportion of people in the lower income levels, for both personal and household income, possibly because a higher proportion had been out of the workforce

The people interviewed for the follow-up study were drawn from the group who specified redundancy/job loss as a trigger for study, with checks to ensure that it was their own experience, rather than that of a spouse, and that their job loss had been involuntary. The interview group consisted of nine women and 12 men, reflecting the closer gender balance of the 'redundancy' group, compared to total respondents. Their average age was 50, with the range from 42 to 56. No one 60 or over was selected for interview to exclude, as far as possible, retirement as a complicating factor. Therefore, all the interviewees were of an age where continuing workforce attachment could be expected.

Almost all the interview group had some postschool qualifications before their recent period of study at Victoria University. Overall, the men had higher qualifications than the women. Six men had degrees and two more part degrees, including three in law and three in science. The others had technical, trade or management qualifications from polytechnics or similar institutions. Among the women, only two had degrees and two had partly completed degrees, all BAs. All the other women had some specialist training, for example in computer or secretarial work. Only one had a technical certificate (electrical engineering) and none had management qualifications. The group therefore represented a typical gender-based pattern of prior educational experience.

Gender differences were evident in the interviewees' work experience, but also considerable career variety. Seven of the men had been in technical occupations, two of whom subsequently become paid officials of trade unions. Two had been private sector managers and two were in the public service. Only one had had a professional career – as an actuary. There was much more variety in the work experience of the women. Only three had professional training – two in teaching. Several had varied careers including secretarial, clerical and retail work.

Experiences of redundancy in midlife

There was considerable variation in how redundancy came about. The male interviewees all reported only one experience, but for four of the women it had happened twice and for one, three times. Information about all the episodes of redundancy is included in the following discussion, but the main focus is on the incident which immediately preceded study at Victoria University.

Table 8.1: Type of redundancy, by gender

Type of redundancy	Male	Female
Personal	1	4
Organisation failure	2	1
Private sector restructuring	2	1
Public sector restructuring	7	3
Total	12	9

Table 8.1 classifies the most recent episodes of redundancy according to their apparent causes. For almost half of the respondents they arose out of public sector restructuring or the disestablishment of a public agency, and for 13 out of 21 from restructuring in either the public or private sectors. These cases, plus those arising from organisation failure, may be classified as external causes, not personal to the interviewee and often beyond his or her control. Personal causes, which appear to have affected women more than men, are situations where the individual was targeted for redundancy because of some personal attribute. The following discussion elaborates on these types of redundancy, through the experiences of the interviewees.

Personal factors
Most of the people affected by redundancy arising from personal factors had not completed professional training and several had worked overseas. Two were 'whistle-blowers'. In one case the interviewee informed higher authorities that a CEO was misappropriating funds. Both had to leave. In the other a teacher protested when owners of a private educational institution began 'ripping off' the students. When she threatened to leave over the situation she was told to go.

In two other cases, workers' conditions were changed drastically and unilaterally, so that they were, in effect, forced out of their jobs. Both women felt there were ageist overtones. Vera took the firm to the employment tribunal and won her case but Dinah felt ashamed and embarrassed and had to be encouraged by her husband to demand a redundancy payment.[1]

Business/organisation failed
There were three instances in which interviewees were made redundant because organisations failed. Todd and Alan had both moved from technical work into jobs as trade union officials. Both unions failed as new industrial legislation took away their statutory rights. Alan realised that he should not have been surprised, but still found the situation unpleasant –

> Everybody was blaming everybody else and at the same time negotiating their own settlements. I had dealt with mass redundancies, but it's completely different when it happens to you.

Alice was running her own art gallery, but in 1995 a series of disasters struck, including a flood, staff problems and a catastrophic rates rise, at the same time as a depression in the art market. Reluctantly she had to close the business and put this experience into the category of redundancy.

Private sector restructuring
Three more interviewees lost their jobs as a result of private sector restructuring, and these were probably the most traumatic examples, although no blame could be laid at the door of the individuals. Bob had worked for 20 years with the same manufacturing company. He knew that a major restructuring was going on and that many employees had

lost their jobs. However, it was still a shock when it happened to him.

> When a certain person came down from head office on the morning flight someone was going to be redundant by the afternoon – this became a joke. But this time it was me. I was summoned to my own office, and given the news then I was off the premises immediately.

William was a branch manager of a large company. The firm was bought out and he 'did not see eye-to-eye' with the new management. He was asked to go to Auckland and told that his position was disestablished. This was totally unexpected, but he thought there was no point in fighting the decision, especially as he was becoming bored with his work – 'a glorified warehouse job'. Karen had been made redundant three times as a result of restructuring in the communications sector. The first two were quite unexpected and hurtful. However, in the third instance, where Karen's work was 'outsourced' she was more in control and felt much better. She could see change coming and even helped with the process.

Public service restructuring
The largest group of interviewees were those who had lost their jobs through public service restructuring, which was rife in New Zealand in the late 80s and early 90s. But within this category are differences based on length and level of employment and how the change was handled. Fred and Adam had each worked for the same agency for about 25 years. When things began to change in the 1990s, Fred became uncomfortable with the new culture. He felt he was being put into situations intended to make him 'blow up and resign' but refused to react.

> They wanted to charge for every cent and cut corners, I really felt it was unprofessional and I was very uncomfortable.

When his manager asked if he would like to be made redundant, it was a shock, but also a release. Adam's experience was similar to that of William and Bob in the private sector. As government policy changed so did his organisation. He knew the exact date –

> On [date], without warning, I was called into the boss's office. There were two other people there that I recognised. I sat down, he read me a statement, passed me a copy and I was just absolutely stunned – I

had been made redundant there and then, without any warning whatsoever. I was given a taxi chit and told to go home. That was it! I had thought I was a key person and didn't suspect anything.

Three people had been in their jobs for 10–15 years, but their experiences of redundancy were very different. Theo could see it coming and could have taken another job. He preferred to be made redundant and receive a 'package' as he had something better to do – he wanted to become a writer. Olivia was not unhappy in her first experience of redundancy as she was pregnant and quite enjoyed being at home. But the second time her section was closed without warning, explanation or possibility of negotiation. Her experience was similar to Karen's. She could accept a situation where she felt she had control, but was hurt and angry when she had none. Joy's section of the public service, she acknowledged, was 'old-fashioned' and probably ripe for change under a new manager. She took redundancy but was apprehensive about her future and felt she lacked the energy to look for a new job.

The rest of the public sector group had been in their jobs for much shorter periods and had had more change in their careers. Most of these could see redundancy coming and some 'jumped before they were pushed'. Kerry's unit was being privatised and, along with other people, he moved onto a contract, with different conditions, to do the same work.

Immediate outcomes and the path to university

The experience of redundancy engendered a variety of reactions. Some of the interviewees had expressed dissatisfaction with their jobs even before they lost them and were happy to go. Others admitted that they had been thinking about a career change, but were still shocked by the actual event. It some cases a feeling of release followed, as in Fred's increasingly difficult work situation. But over half of the group had negative reactions to being made redundant. Some of their feelings were directed externally, as anger towards their employers – feelings of unfairness and frustration. But for others it was a deep personal sense of shame, embarrassment, depression and exhaustion. The women in particular expressed their reactions using terms like miserable, exploited, put down and disempowered.

There was also variety in what happened next, with respect to labour force and educational involvement. About half the interviewees had no significant break in workforce involvement (a matter of weeks rather than months). Some moved into temporary or part-time work or were re-employed on contract. Four people had begun part-time study at university before they were made redundant, pursuing job-related qualifications over a period of years. Five more took up study after redundancy. For seven out of nine, study was related to their previous work. Continuity in work focus, even after the experience of redundancy, did not generally result in a change of direction.

The rest of the interviewees had a break in their workforce participation, extending from several months to a year or more and most of these started university study after a period of unemployment. Some lived on a welfare benefit and some were supported by their spouses or by redundancy money in the meanwhile. Several of this group then became full-time students.

What led members of the redundancy group to take up study at Victoria University? There were three types of motivation. Decisions were made to –

- acquire qualifications needed for progress/re-establishment in their existing career areas
- study in a non-job-related area
- take a new direction in terms of their working careers.

Qualifications in existing career

There were three women in this group and six men. Two of the women enrolled in the Dip.TESOL (teaching English to speakers of other languages). Celia had been teaching untrained in English language schools, but she knew that lack of qualifications had lowered her status and contributed to her two redundancies. Jennifer had a BA and had been teaching at secondary level, but failure to complete her teacher training had dogged her career and she was highly motivated to 'wipe this out'.

> My failure in a teaching course through not completing a minor assignment has cursed me all through my life. Every CV I fill out shows it.

Both women were encouraged to take up their studies by employers. Karen had been taking an extramural Bachelor of Business Studies over several years, while working and having been made redundant three times. In a new job she negotiated help with finance and study leave to work for a Diploma in Information Studies.

Three of the men in this group had begun at university before they were made redundant. All had been in industrial relations work. Todd had acquired most of a BA but did not study for a good while after having been made redundant. The experience made him realise there were areas in his CV which needed 'smartening up' and he needed a postgraduate qualification – 'to compete with the bright young things out of university'. This led him to complete his degree and then a Master's in Public Management. Alan and Pete had begun law degrees before being made redundant. Alan finished his full-time as part of his settlement and went on to do a Master's in law. Pete included history in his degree, but had to resist the temptation to pursue this interest rather than focusing on law – 'I was having too much fun [with history] – I had better concentrate on something more relevant.' None of these three had great difficulty in finding another job and coping with redundancy, perhaps because they had professional knowledge in the area.

The other three men did not have such an easy ride, but still managed eventually to undertake study relevant to their careers. Adam and Jack were already well qualified. Adam had a BCA and professional qualifications. Redundancy hit him hard. For several months he was sending out five or six job applications a week, talking to his contacts, using newspaper and agency sources, without success. He was told he was too old and shamed to be subjected to tests on his English language capacity. After some short-term and part-time work he found his present position. At the same time he embarked on a part-time Master of Financial Mathematics. Jack's experience was similar. When he was made redundant he had just turned 50, with no job to go to and no specific skills. It took him six months to find a job, working his contacts and the agencies and he had begun to get irritable about his lack of success. He had already started a one-off paper before he left his job and thought he needed to fill gaps in his legal knowledge. He started a Master of Law with the idea that it would not only help him to get a job but would also be interesting and therapeutic.

Although William soon found work after his redundancy, he still had a difficult time as he was going through a marital separation and having to find a new home. He had been thinking about studying for a while as he had no credentials to complement his work experience, but he was somewhat in awe of the university. A management consultant advised him to gain a qualification, so when he took up a new job he negotiated time for study as part of his 'package' and enrolled part-time for a diploma in business administration.

Qualifications for a change of career
While some interviewees continued in a career path, with relevant study, others used redundancy as an opportunity for re-evaluation and a change of direction. Sometimes the new career was not too dissimilar to the old, for example from occupational therapy to recreation and leisure studies or from sound recording to communications. For others the jump was more marked. Theo gave up policy analysis for theatre and film courses. Both Fred and Kerry had aspirations in the area of psychology – the former had been a technician and the latter a video editor.

There were some interesting accounts of how redundancy led to a turning point. The three women all experienced stress and exhaustion after their experiences at work and started to ask themselves where they were going. After two experiences of redundancy, at age 41, Olivia went on an Outward Bound course which gave her the opportunity for reflection. This made her realise that she was allowing herself to be manipulated and decided to make her own goals and plans. These included university study. So when her employer would not allow her time for study, she left and enrolled for an MA. 'I have never looked back,' she says.

Dinah was 'willing to do anything' after her redundancy. She received several knock-backs and was told she was too old for a sports administration job. She spent time in voluntary work until her daughter suggested an art history degree. So she enrolled for a BA, part-time in the first instance. Joy did nothing for six or eight months after losing her job. Although she was willing to compromise on pay, no suitable work came her way, but she trained as a Citizen's Advice Bureau volunteer. Like Olivia she began to reflect on her future and read some self-help books. She wanted to do something different, interesting and satisfying, but not in 'an office environment'. Eventually she contacted the university and enrolled for an honours degree in social policy.

The men in this group either did not experience or did not disclose as high a level of stress as the women. Some were fairly matter of fact about their circumstances but others underwent considerable self-searching. Like Olivia and William, Bob had problems in his personal life – his marriage broke up and he was caring for his children. No one wanted his specialised knowledge and there were too many generic managers looking for work. After six months he gave up and became a 'house-husband', enjoying his hobbies and his children 'as most men don't have the opportunity to do'. He thought for a long time about university and then made his mind up and enrolled for a law degree. He called it 'the strangest thing I have ever done' and hoped that law firms would be more forgiving of his age

Fred and Kerry both moved from technical work into psychology. Fred's first aim was to complete his BSc, but he then decided on a change of direction – to 'go as high as I could'. Kerry had been thinking about a career change, but this was easier to put into practice once he was working on contract. Age was beginning to be a problem, he thought. He wanted to move into counselling but found it difficult to get experience, so he began a transitional certificate to prepare for training in clinical psychology.

Non-job-related study
Three women and one man took up study which was not directly related to paid work. After the disastrous closure of her art gallery Alice thought about starting up again, but decided that this would be a step backwards. Instead she went back to university. She already had a degree in English literature and now took on a Master's in art history. This was a continuation of her professional interests, but Alice was clear that there were no job aspirations involved. Vera also had previous experience of university, having begun a BA when she left school. Later, when her daughter was studying, she 'thought it might be fun' to join in. She continued part-time study through two redundancies and a difficult period of marriage break-up and illness. Later she went full-time and added psychology to her study of English.

In contrast, Margot's only previous educational experience was secretarial training at polytechnic. She had always thought that she was not good enough for higher study.

My parents thought you only went to university if you were brilliant or you were going to be a doctor or lawyer. They didn't appreciate knowledge for its own sake.

When her job came to an end she was in her late thirties, all her friends had degrees and she felt she 'wanted to do something different and grow'. A week after leaving her job she started full-time study for a BA in English literature.

Several of the interviewees, as outlined, had personal problems to cope with as well as redundancy. Charles found the death of both his parents harder than losing his job. After a year of trying hard for work, his self-confidence began to decline. His savings were run down, many of his friends deserted him –

No one wanted to know me when I was of no consequence, no longer dressed in a suit and tie.

Like other interviewees, he did voluntary work to 'keep the mind going'. Charles began to think there must be something wrong with him – was it his age or a conspiracy by his former employer? Eventually he decided that it was better to return to university full-time to complete his BSc and then progress to Master's level.

Further outcomes – study, work and personal factors

The interviewees were fairly evenly divided between those who completed their courses at the end of 1999, those who finished in the 2000 academic year and the remainder who were continuing their studies in 2001 or beyond. Thus they varied in how far they could assess the outcomes of their time at Victoria University.

Work
Few of the interviewees who completed their courses in late 1999 had become fully re-established in their jobs or well founded in new careers. After completing his study, Adam eventually found a job as a financial analyst, but did not feel secure and was still on the lookout for jobs, finding it 'frustrating having to compete with younger people'. William completed his postgraduate business diploma and continued as a branch manager, but he also was looking for a different job – to 'stretch' himself. Bob completed his law qualifications, and, after some setbacks was

offered a job in a law firm. But he also felt unsure about his job prospects, because younger people have more 'get up and go'. Among the men who completed in 1999, Dan was the most optimistic. He was setting up his own business and had high hopes.

Olivia, Jennifer and Kerry also completed their courses in 1999 but none had found the work they really wanted. Olivia looked for employment in recreation and leisure but was not successful – 'I think they are predetermined. They have someone in line' – and considered that age discrimination may have been a factor. Eventually she went back to her original work in occupational therapy. Jennifer, with a TESOL diploma and a Master's in applied linguistics, tried hard to find teaching work. Even a refresher course did not help. She settled for private tutoring, but found it very lonely. Her MA appeared too academic for secondary school work and she feared that it still would not override her failed teaching diploma. Finally, among those who completed in 1999, Kerry was waiting to hear if he had been accepted for clinical psychology training and in the meanwhile doing some TV work, plus voluntary work which he hoped would give him counselling experience.

Turning to those who completed their studies in 2000, four people had ongoing full-time jobs which they had acquired following their redundancies. Karen found work as an internal account manager before she completed her postgraduate diploma and felt that she now had much broader experience across the spectrum of business. Alan also found work while he was finishing his Master of Laws, but it was not secure. Both said they had experienced ageism. Alan felt that, given his qualifications, this was the only explanation for his lack of success in the job market. Karen no longer mentioned her age on her CV. Jack had previously held a series of very senior jobs and still headed an organisation, but it had a limited life. However, he preferred to trade off a 'top job' for a lower level of stress. In contrast, Todd was on a career path in the public service as part of his long-term plan, working his way upwards through several changes of job location.

Another group who completed their studies in 2000 had only temporary work. Margot was working in a library part-time, but contemplating a move to another city and probably library training to follow her BA. Celia found work tutoring in a summer course but was content with this as she considered her future. She was no longer sure that she wanted to teach languages – the career which led to two redundancies. Others who had recently completed qualifications were also exploring their options. Theo's ideal was to become a professional writer, but he thought he might combine this with academic work. Going back to his old career as a policy analyst was low on his list. Joy completed her honours degree, but was not looking for full-time work. She wanted to continue with a Master's degree and to work from home as a consultant – an enterprise in which she was having some success. Alice, with her MA in art history had gained some academic recognition and hoped to begin a PhD. She thought the chances of paid employment were not high in her area and at her age. Charles was also considering PhD research. In 2000, he had worked part-time and was also not optimistic about his employment prospects –

It's unlikely that any employer would employ me in anything other than a basic position – a strange situation to be in (at my age).

The other four interviewees had not completed their courses. Pete was working full-time in industrial relations, Vera and Dinah had part-time jobs and Fred had recently begun a PhD in psychology, in his seventh year of study since being made redundant.

Study
Even though the group had not achieved spectacularly in the labour market following the experience of redundancy, most were extremely happy with the outcomes of their study at Victoria University. Looking back, those who had completed their studies talked about enjoying the challenge, extending themselves and building up their self-esteem and confidence. Almost all placed high importance on acquiring a qualification. They found it conferred status and validated their achievements. Dan said, 'People looked at me differently when I'd got my Master's – they listened.' Jack was going to put his Master of Laws certificate on the wall, which he hadn't done with his earlier qualifications –

It's symbolic of my feeling about it – I see it as a final stamp of approval.

Many had ambitions for higher study. Kerry's aspirations to become a clinical psychologist were likely to require three more years of study. Margot was likely to continue library training. But some felt constraints on continuing their university work, deterred by the cost, the time commitment and the pressure. Bob was the only interviewee to mention his age (52) as a constraint to study.

> I found that my memory and eyesight are failing. I had to work harder and to cram it all in before I got too old.

And Vera was the only person to express some ambivalence about her studies. She enjoyed meeting other similar-thinking intelligent people and developed an interest in psychology (as many of the older students seem to do). She wanted to continue with advanced psychology papers but had a setback in early 2000 and sometimes felt 'like I will never finish'.

Personal

In looking back over their recent lives, their experience of redundancy and subsequent university study, the interviewees commented on what it had meant to them in personal terms. They discussed the positive and negative things about education in midlife, frequently referring back to their workforce experience and to events and impressions from much earlier in their lives. The most commonly reported personal changes were increases in confidence, mental stimulation and general awareness. Several reported that they were more critical and analytical about what they did and what went on around them. They also talked about identity. Alice said –

> As I moved into postgraduate study I began to feel as though I was treated like a scholar. I am now seen as more than a housewife – a status denigrated, especially by the next generation. It gives me an identity and makes me more independent.

William spoke at some length about the changes in his life –

> Now I don't feel inferior to people with degrees. I can talk one to one and don't shirk from conversations. I grew a lot, became more confident, more rounded, tolerant and understanding – a better business person. I am not as arrogant as before. I understand people better. I have put things I learned into practice. I have encouraged my staff to learn if it makes them better and gives them more confidence, for example a forklift licence course for warehouse men,

night classes on computers for the ladies. I have knocked a lot of monkeys off my shoulder.

There were also more negative perceptions, usually because circumstantial factors made study harder. For Celia it was lack of financial security combined with age –

> I know I am middle aged and there is a conception that middle-aged people have money. But I feel sick when I think about money. I don't own anything except a $400 computer.

Some interviewees had suffered from ill health and linked this to age. Alan said, 'It isn't worth the intensity of effort working and studying, now I am 50.' Vera cautioned older people about studying – 'it gets harder and harder.' Jennifer felt she was becoming obsessive about her studies, although the pressure was compounded by trouble with her teenage children. These instances illustrate the special strain on all older students, given the context of their lives, with homes, families and the demands of work.

Some of the comment on changes in their personal lives involved family and friends. There were instances where people tried to discourage the interviewees from their studies. Margot's mother was furious with her when she started a degree, doubting that this could lead to a 'proper job' after she had been made redundant. Alice's husband was encouraging but the women in her social circle thought she was 'crazy'. Jack and Pete both had had working class upbringings and talked about proving something to their parents through success in education.

Olivia also cast her mind back to her early educational experience and ascribed her lack of confidence to not having been accredited University Entrance. But, she said – 'I did better than I expected considering where I started.' In contrast, Celia had 'always felt clever' even though she had left school at 16. Now, she says –

> I have it certified. I have a piece of paper which says I am clever.

Several interviewees regretted that they had not been to university earlier, but others, who had achieved more highly in their initial education, commonly they said that they enjoyed their recent study much more because of their greater maturity and insight.

Redundancy – an opportunity or an outrage?

The experience of redundancy was frequently commented on in relation to changes in personal lives. Fourteen out of 21 interviewees clearly identified their experience of redundancy as having been an opportunity to change direction, rethink their lives and take up new challenges, including study at university.

Redundancy could be viewed as positive if it helped people escape from an unhappy environment and a work role where they felt trapped. Bob couldn't afford to leave his management position – 'There are no favours in being well off.' Joy thought that without redundancy she would not have had the courage to move from her humdrum job in the public service. It had been 'a chance to stop the bus and get off'. Looking back, Kerry also felt that he had been resistant to change and Adam appreciated the fact that redundancy had forced him to move out of his 'comfort zone'. Without it he might have stayed in the same job all his working life – 'My wife says it was the best thing that ever happened to me.' Even where they moved quickly to another job, some people could see that the education which followed opened up more stimulation and enjoyment in their careers.

This is not to deny that redundancy can be traumatic enough to qualify as an outrage. William saw it this way, although subsequent study helped to counteract the blow –

> Redundancy knocks back your self-esteem. The effect is longer term that you think. It's like grieving, especially if it is not foreseen. I am thankful I did my education when I did. It was a saviour for me, a lifeline.

Kerry likened redundancy to marriage breakdown – 'It can take away a pillar of your existence' and Todd said – 'If you strongly identify with a job you could lose the will to live' – but fortunately this had not happened to him. Bob changed his views on redundancy in the light of his experience and thought that, if he had not begun his studies previously, he might have been too depressed to start.

> Before it happened to me I wasn't sympathetic to redundant people. I though they were no-hopers. Now I see they can't get themselves out of drugs, booze, behaviour problems. They feel they have nothing left to live for.

Jack also acknowledged that the reaction to redundancy – whether it is seen as an opportunity or an outrage – depended on personal attitudes. He acknowledged that he suffered self-doubt –

> I saw myself as effective and well qualified, but the organisation I had invested so much in didn't want me any more. It was uncomfortable to say I was looking for a job. People wondered what was wrong – embezzlement, breakdown? But university was part of bringing about a new view of life, more relaxed, more considered. If redundancy happens again I could cope.

The remaining seven people did not unequivocally agree that their experience of redundancy had been an opportunity. This was their view, although an external evaluation might see their situation differently. Some of this group had been studying already and did not have a major break in their paid work. The main motivation for study for Celia and Jennifer had been a growing realisation that they did not have the necessary teaching qualifications. But having been made redundant certainly clarified and exemplified their position.

Even if they did not clearly recognise redundancy as an opportunity, comments from this group echoed those of the group who did. Karen and Fred pondered where they might have been had the redundancy not happened – respectively 'in a dead end job' and 'pottering on until retirement'. Charles's comments could be seen as contradictory. He said that redundancy was not an opportunity or a trigger, but lack of a job for several months afterwards was. And he agreed that he would not have gone back to university if he had not been made redundant.

This group also acknowledged the change that they had experienced since redundancy. Olivia felt that her confidence had been 'healed' by her time at university and she was determined not to be exploited again. Fred said he now had so many possibilities open to him. He was 'coming back to life' (after redundancy and the death of his first wife). So even among those who were not clear that redundancy had been an opportunity, similar perceptions emerge, clearly linking the experience with university study and consequent positive change.

Conclusion

Many common themes arise from this analysis of the stories of 21 people who were students at Victoria University after having experienced redundancy. They came from a wide variety of backgrounds, levels and types of work and educational achievement. For the most part, redundancy arose from restructuring in their workplaces – sometimes it was predictable and sometimes not. Some interviewees were already thinking about movement and others were aware of their need for qualifications in a changing work environment. But, even so, for almost everyone redundancy was still a shock and often produced feelings of anger, shame and depression.

Having experienced redundancy, most of the group faced problems of adjustment in their working and personal lives. Apart from exhaustion and depression, they were aware of competition from well-qualified and energetic younger people and recognised that their age might well be against them. Several experienced overt ageism in the process of losing their jobs and as they looked for new positions.

Where there was a clear gap between leaving one job and finding another, this provided the opportunity for reassessment and a possible change of direction. Some interviewees decided to complete qualifications already started, some to acquire the credentials they needed for progress and others to realise dreams of alternative careers or interest-based study, which they may have been developing for years.

The analysis shows that reestablishment in paid work was not easy for the group. Many had only temporary or part-time work or jobs with which they were not satisfied, even a year after they graduated. Some were resigned, but others were still ambitious. Despite very mixed success in the work arena, however, there was agreement that the decision to study had been a positive move. The interviewees had grown in confidence, self-esteem and general awareness. Their view of the world and of themselves had changed. University study had been a means of personal growth and of counteracting the blow of redundancy.

Despite the negative effects of losing their jobs, often in a traumatic and hurtful way, the experience of redundancy could also be an opportunity, as shown in these accounts. There is no information, from a total population perspective, on how many people take up educational opportunities after redundancy. University study cannot be offered as a general panacea and the acquisition of academic qualifications is not always the best career move. However, the stories of the nine women and 12 men who shared their experiences in the 'Education in Mid and Later Life' project show that it can be a valuable and positive option.

Notes

1   The interviewees have been given pseudonyms to protect their confidentiality.

9

UNIVERSITY STUDY IN RETIREMENT – CONTINUITY, SUBSTITUTION AND IDENTITY

Judith A Davey

Why do people in their sixties and beyond become university students? The majority of the 40-plus students at Victoria had work-related motives for their study. Surely these are left behind once people retire? Theories of human ageing can be useful in approaching these questions. Status in western societies is mostly achieved through occupational prestige. After retirement this is difficult to maintain. The 'identity crisis' theory of retirement, suggests that loss of occupational identity accompanying retirement can be socially debilitating.[1] This assumes that paid work is the dominant factor in identity and personality and that lost roles cannot be replaced. It is also a very male interpretation of changes surrounding retirement and underestimates continuity in other aspects of life such as family, friendship, unpaid and community work, leisure and learning. Few people rest their entire identity on a single role. The alternative identity continuity theory suggests that people seek substitutes for activities left behind by ageing. Social contacts with family and friends or new activities such as leisure and education may be substituted, serving the same needs for self-esteem and self-enhancement.[2] Following the theme of substitution, Ekerdt suggested that the work ethic may be replaced by the 'busy ethic' as part of the transition to retirement.[3] Strands of life from the past may be resumed, interwoven and adapted. Substitution and continuity theory therefore provide an alternative to the 'disengagement theory', which gives a somewhat negative view of ageing.

What experiences and knowledge can people draw from to make these selections and adaptations? Work history, both paid and unpaid work, is one influence. Family history is another important source of continuity, including class-based attitudes and expectations.[4] Historical and social events such as wars and economic recessions as well as prevailing social and cultural norms all have their effect. This chapter examines how the study choices and experiences of 60-plus students at Victoria University have been influenced by their previous life histories and how university study can contribute to the maintenance of a positive identity in retirement.

The 60-plus group at Victoria University

People aged 60 and over represented only 5% of the 40-plus students at Victoria University and only one in every 300 students as a whole. Forty-nine responded to the postal survey and of these 21 were interviewed – 15 women and six men, with ages ranging from 60 to 82.[5] The interviewees were selected on the basis of being retired from their career work and either out of the workforce or working only part-time. The gender balance is rather more even than among the 40–59 age group at Victoria University, probably because men are more likely to study at university once they are retired, but women still predominate. The 60-plus group among Victoria students was typical of the age group in the total population in respect of ethnicity (being very predominantly Pākehā) and household circumstances. A higher proportion of the men were living with a partner, while the women were more likely to be living alone. Only two people lived with people other than their spouse.

Family of origin and initial education

The interviewees' experiences with initial education, dating back in the main to the 1930s and 1940s, were varied and did not always follow expected class lines. Seven were early school leavers, who left either without qualifications or with only School Certificate. Three began 'on-the-job' or apprenticeship-type training. Four continued straight into bachelors degrees – two BAs, one Bachelor of Engineering, one law degree – and two more started degree courses straight from school but did not finish them at this stage. Five went into some type of professional training, including nursing and teaching.

Three early school leavers came from clearly working-class families, but others had fathers in middle-class occupations such as post office official, accountant and shopkeeper. Other interviewees came from humble backgrounds but still went straight on into university or professional training. May's father was a boilermaker but she trained as a nurse. Don's father abandoned his family when Don was three, but he still managed to become articled to an accountant.

Of the five who went straight to university from school and the two who went into teacher training, four clearly came from 'middle-class' or professional families. Joan's father was a secondary teacher; both Grace's parents were school inspectors; Laura followed her father into law and John followed his into professional engineering. Two more were from farming families.

Attitudes towards continuing at school beyond the minimum leaving age have been associated with class, which was certainly the case for Geraldine and Katherine. Geraldine was one of 11 children of a stevedore and a barmaid, brought up in the north of England. Although she passed the exam to go to grammar school, she left at the minimum age. She got a job doing routine clerical work and this was considered vastly superior to the alternative of working in a dye factory. Neither of Katherine's parents had any secondary education. She gained School Certificate, but left at 16 because her brother was starting that year and her parents could not afford to support them both. Her mother was against her being a nurse and she could not train for secondary teaching, as she would have liked, because she had no University Entrance, so she took up typing.

But gender expectations prevalent at the time could cut across class. Sheila's father was an accountant and she stayed at a private girls' school until the 6th form. Her parents didn't think that education was important for a girl.

> I was not allowed to become a blue stocking, they thought I would not attract men.

Parental aspirations could sometimes be more encouraging. Some working-class parents were ambitious for their children's education. For example, Trevor's father was a farm worker and his mother a gloving outworker. When he passed his scholarship for grammar school there was debate about whether he should take up this opportunity. His father thought he ought to go to work – further education would be too expensive. However, his mother disagreed and, as she was the money manager, her view prevailed.

Decisions about leaving school and further education were influenced not only by parental attitudes, but also by peer pressure and work opportunities. In the 1950s and 60s in New Zealand there was a labour shortage, jobs were easy to obtain and replace if they did not suit. Young people, especially males, often travelled around the country, moving from job to job. Stan was one of these –

> I wanted to get away from [the small South Island town where he had been brought up]. I took off and travelled around the North Island on my OE [overseas experience].

There were other important contextual factors. The oldest of the interviewees was born in 1918 and the youngest in 1940. Those who are now in their 80s were brought up before the full range of welfare state provisions was developed. This affected their educational and other opportunities. Deirdre's parents broke up before she was five and she and her two siblings were sent to an orphanage as, in the absence of any sole parent benefits (except for widows), their mother had to find paid work. This was not an uncommon event at the time. When she left school at 14 her options were limited and she took a live-in job as a child-minder.

The Second World War affected many of the interviewees and either set back or diverted their educational prospects. Rose's father was killed when she was four. Her mother was left very poorly off with three girls to rear. So Rose had to leave school and go to work, She cried as she left school, as she had always wanted to go to university. Nina was in a country occupied by enemy troops and her education ceased for six years. At the end of the war she tried to catch up, but there was a severe shortage of teachers and she started to work in a primary school.

Grace and Chris were nearing school leaving age when the war began. Grace's parents wanted her to go to university, but she opted for teacher training to give her more time for war work. Chris had intended to move on to a law degree but instead he left school at 17, joined the army and did two years of condensed officer training. Before the end of the war, at age 19, he was with an engineering corps in Italy.

Subsequent education

Despite leaving school at minimum age or soon after, all seven early school leavers went on to do further formal study. All the women subsequently gained a university degree. Typically, this was in their late thirties at the earliest, when they had completed their families and the heaviest demands of child rearing were past. Rose did her University Entrance exams in her thirties and began a BA at age 39. Geraldine also did school-level exams through evening classes and followed this with a journalism course before she began university at age 42. Rae and Katherine did degrees in their 50s and Deirdre had been retired for several years before she started on the track which would eventually lead her (from an orphanage) to doctoral studies.

Those who went on to tertiary study straight from school did not necessarily remain attached to learning. Among those with very long gaps in their education experience were Laura and Sheila. Laura added some language courses to her law degree, but did no other study from her early twenties until well after her retirement. Sheila completed four units of accountancy immediately after school, but also did not go back to formal study until she left work.

For several interviewees, especially the men, ongoing study was encouraged as part of their careers, so it was easy for them to continue in education. Examples include Trevor in personnel management and industrial relations; Chris (army), Carl (church ministry) and several of the female teachers. Others, however, made a personal effort to study. Lillian abandoned her MA when she married, but took extramural papers while she was at home with her children. Joan gave up her music degree for similar reasons, but took continuing education music courses and piano classes while caring for her family.

Retirement and postretirement education

Fifteen of the interviewees considered themselves retired. The others described themselves variously as a writer, community worker, student, house parent and two as tutors. The average age at retirement was 63. The only person to retire before 60 was Laura. She left work to have more time with her mother, who was failing in health. The experience of retirement was variable. Some interviewees reached the set retirement age for their workplace or negotiated an agreed time with their employers. Four were pleased to leave their career jobs because they did not like the changes occurring in their public sector workplaces. Others were less willing to give up their career work. Diana left teaching at the age of 63 after feeling pressure from her colleagues who thought that younger people needed the work more. Grace remained in distance education until she was 72, when a requirement to upskill seemed like a signal to go.

How did study at Victoria University fit in with the timing of retirement? Some people started their courses very soon after retirement, but others delayed their studies for several years. For Deirdre the trigger was the death of her husband, when she was 73. She picked up correspondence courses the next year and university study the year after. Nina migrated to New Zealand after retirement and was soon taking evening classes in Japanese and French. It was only 8 years after retirement that she followed the example of her grandchildren and began a BA.

Other activities took most of three male interviewees' attention immediately after retirement. Stan and Chris became very involved in golfing and the Probus club, respectively, and both became high office-holders. It was only when these activities became less onerous that formal study could begin. Carl retired from his career job, but was busy developing training courses for the next 12 years.

Four interviewees were already studying at university level at the time of retirement. For John and May this was overtly 'in anticipation of retirement'. For the rest of the interviewees, setting their university studies in the context of retirement is problematic as they did not consider themselves retired. However all were working only part-time and had either left or did not have a career job.

Choices

Why university study? Many of the interviewees who had not previously attended university expressed a long-held desire for study at this level, and for those who had been before it was an obvious choice as a venue for learning. Several people had tried distance learning but found it isolating and others were not satisfied by community-based classes. There were several comments on the University of the Third Age (U3A) courses, which were seen as low level and non-participatory.

Why study at all and why this subject? These two questions are difficult to separate. For some interviewees the answer was a desire to pursue an interest of very long standing – either work related, a hobby, or an aspect of personal experience. Given that most of the interviewees are retired, work-related interests were not to the fore, although the choice of courses sometimes related back to previous careers.

Building on a long-term hobby was the motive for John in embarking on a Bachelor of Music. He had been playing the clarinet for 30 years and now he was retired he wanted to know more about the technical aspects of music so that he could arrange music for his group of amateur players. Lillian's interest in art sprang originally from a paper on the Renaissance which was part of her history degree in the 1950s.

For some interviewees, the desire to study arose out of a comparatively recent interest. Trevor's developed almost accidentally, as he saw it. Going to a recreational class on Polynesian dance led to university courses in Pacific languages and then into a BA in anthropology and linguistics. Three years after her retirement, Diana went on a continuing education tour to Greece and Italy but was frustrated that she did not know more about what she was seeing. She went back to complete a degree in classics the next year, building on university credits done at the time of teacher training in 1940s. After her retirement, and failing to find the part-time work she was seeking, Sheila started work on a book on commercial history. However, she 'needed a place to go' and began a BA in history.

Previous life experiences provided the impetus for some people. For Chris, Nina and May this was their time in other countries. Chris went back to Italy to see people and places which he knew from the war and returned with a strong interest in learning Italian. Nina and May both chose Asian studies, building on their experiences of living overseas.

For several women, their most recent period of study represented a natural progression from earlier academic work. Laura picked up from her 1940s studies in Latin and German and this led to an MA and then a PhD. When Geraldine moved into tutoring, after completing an honours degree in English and philosophy, she was told she needed an MA. Rae was working on an MA in women's studies, which she was encouraged to do this after completing her BA in her 40s, following the breakdown of her marriage.

Three other women had achieved undergraduate degrees before retirement and simply gave continuing general interest as their motive for further study. For example, Grace completed her first BA (English literature and art history) after she retired and started postgraduate

English, but she found her lack of computer skills a drawback and gave up. Instead she decided to do a second BA in classical studies. The university authorities demurred at this, but Grace was firm – 'when you are 76 you know what you want to do.'

The role of study in retirement

How did study fit into life in retirement? Did it provide a substitute for paid work? Several of those interviewed were clear that study provided structure in their lives. Katherine worked regular hours on her thesis on week days, punctuated by walks and a regular weekly shopping trip. Deirdre had a work schedule, with breaks to buy a paper, do the crossword, meditate, walk and have a snooze. She said 'I have a routine and am a nervous wreck if I am interrupted.' Some of the interviewees clearly saw university study as a job substitute –

> Study gives structure to life. I would have been lost for the first two to three years of retirement without it. (Rose)

> After working for so long I could get lazy, so it's good to have a routine. I go in four times a week – I just do it. (Susan)

> The university is 'my club'. I come in most days and spend time socialising in the quad. I sit in front at lectures and meet older students that way. (Don)

The concept of study as a substitute for work can be carried further. Where people filled their lives with activity in retirement, they actually granted themselves 'holidays' from it. When he was interviewed, John was enjoying 'a wonderful year off studying'. Like paid work before retirement, the demands of study, even though freely chosen, can become almost onerous. Diana hinted at this –

> Study does give structure to my life and this is important. I like the lectures, having lunch with people, getting out of the house, even the trip in to university by bus. It is good to understand what people are doing, not to feel shut out of the world. But sometimes it's a bit like slavery.

When Laura left work she was free to concentrate on study as she had no family and lived alone. Her university work came to dominate her life and although it provided structure and stimulation, she felt it may have crowded out other activities. Susan also thought that her social life had been reduced, especially when she had university assignments to complete. Joan noticed the same effect, but actually preferred study to social life – 'I get impatient just meeting friends in town.' Diana likened the completion of her degree to a second retirement, which she was sure she would manage better than her first.

Family and caring work occupied time in several of the interviewees' lives and, although it was mostly seen positively, this also competed with other activities. Several of the female interviewees mentioned caring for their grandchildren. Deirdre had 17 grandchildren, and those who live nearby visited her daily. They added to the interruptions to her study, which she found so bothersome, but she cooperated to gain the social contact. Rose's grandchildren also frequently came to stay – 'I feel guilty when I have to say no to them when I have an essay due.'

Don was the only interviewee caring for a child. He anticipated feeling depressed when his daughter leaves home, but expected to 'switch to pottering around the university'. Grace was caring for her husband, who was severely limited by arthritis. She fitted her study around his needs. She called it 'working in the cracks'.

All these examples show how people felt the need to remain busy in retirement, substituting study and other activities for career occupations, with overtones of a moral imperative. Nina made this clear –

> I don't find happiness in gambling [playing mah-jong] as my peers do. It's a waste of time, I would rather read. Study gives me an aim and something to look forward to.

Experience of university study

Once at university, the 60-plus students faced a range of both negative and positive factors, which impinged on their view of themselves in the roles of students and retired people.

Only three of the interviewees felt that there were no barriers to them achieving their study objectives. They were mainly time constraints – barriers which the group shared with 40-plus students as a whole. Several commented about travel and parking, especially those who lived some distance from Victoria. 'A whole day virtually spent to attend one lecture, at most two,' complained Chris.

Only two people mentioned money as a barrier to study. Half of the interviewees made no comment about personal funding problems, but several commented generally that study was an expensive business for retired people. Chris felt that expenses had to be prioritised – 'A consideration is to rank the cost of study in priority with other household expenditure'. There were three comments about student loans or problems with them. Six of the interviewees had funded their studies partly through student loans. In New Zealand there is no upper age limit for student loans, which are written off at death.

Institutional barriers, arising from university systems and facilities, were sometimes mentioned. Diana complained about library restrictions and John about a shortage of computers. Some of the postgraduate students were having problems with supervision.

> It has taken so long to get the second examiner's report in for my thesis. I feel disappointed, isolated and frustrated – it has already taken some of the shine off. (Cynthia)

Such problems for postgraduate students are not, of course, confined to older people.

Thus far, the barriers mentioned were shared by adult students in general. Dispositional barriers were more clearly age related. Students aged 60-plus were more likely to mention health problems, less effective memory and lower energy levels than the 40–59 age group. Among the interviewees it was mainly the women who mentioned physical factors. Katherine found it hard to climb uphill to some of the classrooms. Rose and Sheila complained of lack of energy and arthritis. It was the men in particular who suggested mental disadvantages, especially poorer memory, slower and less reliable thinking processes. As a result, examinations were almost universally seen as extremely stressful and difficult.

> The head doesn't work quite as well as it used to. (Trevor)

> Older people are not as quick, more anxious, worry a lot. (Joan)

In the 'Education in Mid and Later Life' postal survey all respondents were asked if they thought there were disadvantages in studying in later life. For those aged 60 or older about 70% thought that there were. This is lower than the 75% figure for the 40-plus students as a whole, indicating a slightly more positive view among the older group. Despite the high proportion who cited disadvantages for older students, an even higher percentage thought that there were advantages, including almost all of the 60-plus group. Life experience was especially stressed. This could bring greater tolerance and breath of vision. Among the comments was Rose's –

> Older students bring life experience – they can see more of what authors are on about, how their minds work. Young ones are quicker and brighter and do get As, but they have tunnel vision. They see everything in black and white.

Mention of confidence and maturity increased with age among the survey respondents.

> Fewer distractions, ability to focus more, hormonal level zilch and I can spell. (May)

Katherine considered that older students were more relaxed and had more fun. Don and John thought they could get on better with the university staff. Rae said that study keeps you mentally alert – 'otherwise you would seize up like an old car.' In a more practical vein, several interviewees mentioned that 60-plus students had more time and fewer family demands to cope with. However these barriers were not completely absent, as already shown.

Stan and Chris were the only interviewees who did not agree that older people had advantages as students.

> I envy the youngsters who are fresh from a good secondary school. (Stan)

> I do not consider the university is well geared for older students. Its main preoccupation is with youth. (Chris)

There were a few comments about attitudes towards older people at university. Some felt a lack of opportunity to draw upon their experience or have opinions respected. Others found that relationships with younger lecturers could be difficult –

> You can seem presumptuous and making things difficult. (Chris)

> Young people are embarrassed to tell older people what to do or feel they will become domineering. (Don)

Only Geraldine, however, felt that she had suffered seriously from ageism and sexism.

Members of staff do not take one as seriously as younger students. Mentoring is not as available for older students in my experience.

Thus, apart from appreciating the physical and mental effects of old age, in terms of health, mobility and memory, the 60-plus students do not perceive any greater barriers to educational involvement than people in the 40–59 age group, and their attitudes are equally positive.

Feelings about university study

Recalling their university experiences, the people who were interviewed typically reported a sequence of emotions.

Apprehension
Most of the 60-plus students found university as they had expected. However, this did not mean that all approached the institution with confidence. Several were very unsure of themselves and their abilities at first. Lillian and Stan feared that their study skills would be out of date. Geraldine had thought 'you had to be very clever – super intelligent – to go to university'. Frequently this was related to their age and the feeling that they would not 'fit in' with the school leavers at Victoria University.

Adjustment
As the older people moved into their courses, many of their fears proved unfounded. They adjusted and began to enjoy both their study and their interactions with younger and mature students.

I have been treated as 'normal' by students and staff and in no way patronised. To me this was a surprise and a delight. (Stan)

You have to make an effort to fit it, not to take over in seminars, to listen. But the younger students were very tolerant and I have met some wonderful mature students. (Lillian)

Nevertheless, where the older students live at a distance and/or study only part-time, they may have little interaction with other students and find it difficult to integrate. When asked about satisfaction with features of university experience, the highest levels of dissatisfaction, expressed by the interviewees and the postal survey respondents, were with their relationships with other students.

Joy
Joy and excitement clearly shone through the words of the interviewees when they spoke about their study experiences, especially the women.

> It's a lot of fun and I am having a wonderful time. I get more of an adrenaline rush with this research than with any job I could go for at my stage of life. (Katherine)

> It's magic – I really like history. People said 'you're drooling'. I came away angry with dead teachers who only told us one side of the story. Study is addictive – now that it is over I am grieving. (May)

> I found it liberating, exciting. In fact I need to get less excited. I fizz along too much. (Lillian)

> It's really heady stuff. Study has become a way of life. I can't put it down. (Joan)

> I almost felt like clapping in some of the lectures. (Stan)

Others were a little more measured in their reactions, but still talked about the pleasure of learning, the new vistas which their studies had opened up for them, the challenges, but also the stimulation when their abilities met the test.

Confidence and self-esteem
Despite barriers and difficulties, for the majority of respondents university study ultimately became a source of confidence, respect and credibility and a boost to their identity as retired people. Even those who had lacked self-confidence initially, like Geraldine and Lillian, began to feel they were proving themselves. In his music course, John was forced, not only to compose a piece, but to sing his own song. He rose to the occasion –

> They got me doing things I never thought I would.

Interviewees were proud to report on the respect which study gave them and on their families' support. Diana's children all had degrees and her husband was a retired scientist, still active in his field. She liked to feel that she was keeping up with him in her own way. Stan's pleasure in learning was reinforced by knowing that 'not only my children can do well'. Grace talked about her granddaughter who is studying at another university –

> She looks to me as an example, and says 'Grace, I like to see you doing that.' I think I encourage them, by obviously enjoying my study.

Cynthia also said her husband was secretly quite pleased at her achievements. She said jokingly – 'He thinks it's a bit of a hoot!' – but also felt that the satisfaction was shared by all her family. Nina felt that she was part of a family tradition of valuing education. All of her five children and now her ten grandchildren were well educated.

> It shows my children and grandchildren that I am one of them. They tell people 'my grandmother is at the university'.

Sheila summed up the pride in their achievements which infused many of the 60-plus students.

> I am incensed when people just say, 'I am doing some papers at Vic.' *I* say, 'I am "working for a BA".' People say, 'Are you really?' I like that. I have a new persona – university student.

This is not to suggest that everyone in the group enjoyed such support. May's daughter was horrified when her mother started her BA. But her grandchildren were delighted and boasted about it. Others found their friends disinterested or even critical, but their confidence allowed them to ignore such attitudes.

> Most of my friends think I am nuts. (Susan)

> My friends almost sneered. They thought it wouldn't last and said I would be bored. A lot of people still don't know that I go to university; I try not to talk about it. (Stan)

Indulgence

For several of the interviewees, both men and women, the pleasure and satisfaction which they derived from study brought almost guilty feelings of selfishness. Grace considered that she was being 'wickedly self-indulgent', Deirdre that she was 'egotistical and self-centred'. These feelings were linked with a somewhat puritanical view that it could not be quite right to enjoy something so much or that time should be spent in more altruistic pursuits. To counteract the feeling, interviewees frequently expressed the view that studying is good for older people, providing stimulation and structure in retirement. John's mother died of Alzheimer's disease. He was clear in his view that senile decay is staved off by activity.

Satisfaction
Thus, looking back over their university experience, the interviewees mostly expressed high levels of satisfaction. All were satisfied or very satisfied with the choice of courses and course content. Rae and Geraldine expressed some dissatisfaction with teaching and assessment and two others felt that the level of teaching quality had been 'mixed'. Four interviewees were dissatisfied with their own performance at university and three neutral. Lillian and Stan felt that they were not thinking as quickly as when they were younger, but Joan was realistic – 'Study is addictive, one always wants to do better.' Despite this the majority of interviewees were satisfied with their own performance.

Outcomes of study in retirement

Apart from a boost to confidence and self-esteem, what else emerged from the experiences of the 60-plus group at Victoria University?

Gaining a qualification
It has been assumed that older learners are not interested in qualifications, grades and competition.

> Unlike education for the young, education for the older adult is not perceived as a necessity for the maintenance of society. From this credential-obsessed perspective, old people may pursue education, but it is strictly a private pursuit for leisure-time activity, with no larger meaning or purpose.[6]

This assumption does not ring true in the Victoria University study. Even when they are no longer in paid work people may want qualifications to prove something to themselves, for personal accomplishment and satisfaction. As shown already in comments regarding self-esteem, some people certainly set store by gaining a qualification. This was sometimes for themselves –

I achieved more than I expected of myself. It's the satisfaction of achieving a degree and pleasure of study. Without a purpose I would rot away. I don't fuss about my doctorate, but it is a great source of satisfaction. (Laura)

The qualification is not important but it is important to finish for my self-esteem. Now I have started [a PhD] I would feel I was not achieving if I didn't complete it, especially as many people know I am doing it. (Katherine)

Sometimes for others –

It is important to my husband that I get a qualification. It adds to the significance of what I am doing. He benefits too – it gives him status. (Grace)

A smaller group, however, felt that the degree was not an end in itself –

Many underestimate what older people want from education and think that U3A is enough. Qualifications may be important for some. For me 'getting there' is what is important. (Joan)

A BA is not important but I can't see the point of flogging your way up there [to university] without there being something at the end. A serious person needs an objective. (Sheila)

Or even that it had become devalued –

It is not important for me to get a degree – a BA doesn't have the aura it had years ago. It means nothing now, it's not rare. (Chris)

Further study

Many of the interviewees had considered themselves to be 'not very bright', in Trevor's words, but proved otherwise. Several said they regretted not having studied more when they were younger. But this did not deter several of those who had recently completed a qualification from further study. For example, Chris was seeking to move out from language study into more abstract and (to him) more challenging areas such as philosophy and linguistics. However, all had some reservations, in terms of their abilities, energy and financial resources.

Those who ruled out further study either had failing health, or caring responsibilities such as Grace. But even here the door was not closed. 'I'll see how I manage after a year off,' said Diana. 'I would like to do honours or an MA, but not now,' said Grace.

Advice to other older students
The postal questionnaire respondents were asked what advice they would give to other older people contemplating university study. The overall response was to offer unequivocal encouragement and this was the same for the 60-plus interviewees. Half unreservedly encouraged their peers. 'Do it now. You don't get any younger,' said Katherine. 'Go for it. Life begins at university. You can do it!' was May's enthusiastic exhortation.

Some offered a rider to their encouragement –

Do it, but be aware of the commitment of time, energy and money it involves. Personally I have found the experience deeply enriching personally and intellectually. (Geraldine)

Others, including most of the male interviewees, pointed out the personal attributes which would be required – commitment, perseverance, determination, hard work and sacrifice. Several offered practical advice to other older students, all related to study.

Learn to work 'in the cracks'. Keep going even if tired and discouraged. Be very systematic in keeping notes or research items together. Use cardboard boxes, envelopes, and plastic bags if you can't afford a computer or files. (Grace)

Never get behind in your work. Ask lots of questions; seek staff help as soon as you need it. Don't get distracted. (John)

Conclusion

Continuity
The lives and educational experiences of the 21 interviewees clearly illustrate aspects of continuity and substitution theory. However, there appear to be several types of continuity.

•   First is continuity through close association with education.

Several interviewees either came from families where parents were involved in education or were teachers themselves and strongly imbued with the value of learning. The considerable representation of teachers among the female interviewees reflects the limited career choices available for academically oriented girls in the 1940s and 1950s. Teacher training was frequently chosen, by parents and students, rather than university courses.

- For a group of interviewees, parental support and/or their own choices led them to stay on at school and continue their studies directly afterwards, thus setting them on a trajectory which predisposed them to continuing educational involvement. In some cases, this initial tertiary study promoted a non-job-related interest which was returned to much later in life.

- Some interviewees periodically returned to work-related education and training. This did not mean that they continued their subject interest into later life – work-related areas were generally left behind at retirement – but work-related education habituated them to study. This type of continuity applied especially to male members of the group.

- A further type of continuity arose from strong personal interests or experiences which fuelled the desire to learn and to study at university level. These could be an active hobby or cultural pursuit or an interest in culture in the ethnic sense.

- Much less tangible is continuity which stems from personal attitudes. Several interviewees, all women, described their lifelong interest in learning as part of their personality. For example, Rose came from a poor, fatherless family and was not encouraged to go to university even though she was a 'scholarship girl'. She said –

I don't know where my ambition came from. I found the library myself at age eight and found classical music at age 11. I became addicted to reading. When I wasn't allowed to take a book to the meal table I used to read the labels on the sauce bottles.

Grace also felt that the instinct was deeply ingrained in her personality. Her whole family saw education as a way of helping people. She said –

Loving and caring about people and doing my job well is very
important. My college motto was – Serve Joyfully . . . Does that
sound soppy?

Others drew on their personal resources to persevere with their
educational interests despite discouragement. For example, Joan came
from an academic background, but had to leave university after one
year because of her father's illness. She later had an unhappy marriage
and more than her share of family tragedy. Nevertheless she felt that
for her study was a way of life, and she has moved steadily through
degree levels until she was contemplating a PhD. Rae's background had
some similarities, although her initial education was rudimentary and
she never developed a 'career' as such. She also had an unhappy marriage
and family tragedy. In the wake of this she sought to improve her
prospects and is now working on an MA.

The 'busy ethic'

The analysis of interviews with the 60-plus students shows that the 'busy
ethic' is alive and well among this group. Their studies clearly promoted
a good self-image and raised self-esteem. Levels of enjoyment and
fulfilment were high. For the people involved, study did indeed
substitute for paid work, not only in providing structure to life in
retirement, but also in imparting purpose and prestige.

In the eyes of the older students themselves, study served a valuable
purpose in keeping them engaged, active and interested, avoiding
boredom and stagnation and, at least to some extent, counteracting
stereotypes of older people. Mixing with younger people at university
was important in achieving this. Thus, educational involvement can
indeed be seen as assisting the transition to retirement and contributing
to successful ageing in the psychological sense.

Two final points must be borne in mind. Firstly, we must
acknowledge the atypicality of older university students. Those who
undertake university study past retirement tend to be the more
determined and disciplined, with more education than the rest of their
age group. It would not be realistic to expect that all older people could
achieve successful ageing through high-level study. However, as
educational levels rise among the on-coming age cohorts there will be
more and more people aged 60 and older who will have the background,
experience and capacity to undertake university study. This leads to

the second point, which is to stress the importance of diversity among the retired population. To accept that education has a role in the promotion of positive ageing is not to imply that 'one size fits all' in terms of provision. Ideally a variety of educational opportunities will be offered. Joan has the last word –

Diversity is important. U3A for some, research degrees for others.

Notes

1 Atchley (1989).
2 Midwinter (1998), Young and Schuller (1991).
3 Ekerdt (1986).
4 Harevan and Adams (1982), Jerrome (1994).
5 In this chapter the interviewees have all been given pseudonyms for reasons of confidentiality.
6 Pifer and Bronte (1986).

10

WHY DO THEY LEAVE? – MATURE STUDENTS AND WITHDRAWAL FROM STUDY

Jenny Neale

Introduction

Withdrawal from study is an area of concern for all those involved with students at university. As McInnis indicates, every student who withdraws early from study, especially if dissatisfied, is a problem for the credibility of tertiary education.[1] There has been particular emphasis on the first-year experience. Research indicates that besides those who leave at the end of their first year there are others whose leaving in the second and sometimes third year has its roots in the first-year experience.[2] The faculty of health sciences at the University of Sydney, for example, found that 25% of their first-year students had seriously contemplated withdrawal.

A number of factors leading to early withdrawal have been identified. In particular there are the structural problems that inhibit the first-year experience – the lack of interactive opportunities (a view reinforced by surveys of nine US and Canadian institutions, and the wide use of the Student Adaptation to College Questionnaire), little opportunity for oral communication and feedback, no identification with the institution, increased class sizes and lecture-dominated teaching, which lead to a sense of alienation and isolation. A 1994 Australian study by Craig McInnis, Richard James, and Carmel McNaught[3] has also highlighted concerns about teaching quality, a lack of enthusiasm among staff and inadequate feedback. Academics' attitudes towards the status of teaching compared with research, increased workload and decreased resources, and insufficient time, particularly with increased internal assessment, and the tension between vocational education and liberal education were further inhibiting factors.

Other factors were related to financial problems, and the parallel need to be in paid employment for high numbers of hours. Astin highlights the negative effects of part-time work (unless on campus) and indicates that this can seriously impact on completion, cultural awareness, knowledge, preparation for graduate study and satisfaction. Yorke et al also related non-completion to the demands of employment while studying. A 30-year trend analysis across the USA indicates that students are now spending more time in paid employment and socialising with friends and less time studying.[4] A survey in Britain indicated that one in six students were dropping out of degree courses. Further research will investigate whether rising indebtedness, fees and abolition of grants have led to this.[5]

Method

My research on withdrawal from university study draws on data from two groups of students. Of the 959 mature students who replied to the 'Education in Mid and Later Life' postal survey, over 700 indicated a willingness to be involved further in the research. As the earlier chapters in this book indicate, a number were followed up and interviewed in depth. In the process of recontacting prospective interviewees, these mature students were also asked if they had withdrawn before completing their study. When this was the case, permission was gained to carry out a brief withdrawal questionnaire. Subsequently, all those who were unable to be included in the interviews because of time and financial constraints were sent four core questions and a copy of the withdrawal questionnaire. These two approaches produced 77 replies (around 10% of those who had indicated interest in further contact) from mature students who had withdrawn from study before completing the qualification they initially sought.

Secondly, as part of a longitudinal study of a cohort of full-time first-year students at Victoria University in 1996, those who did not continue for a second year were followed up. Eighty phone interviews were completed with these former students. No one who was contacted refused to take part.

The withdrawal questionnaire for both surveys was based on one developed by Jim Elliot at Curtin University in Australia. Using the same questionnaire enabled us to compare the data from the two groups of students at Victoria University as well as providing a further comparison with the Australian data. As the Elliot questionnaire was administered to students leaving in the first semester of study, adaptations were made for the initial Victoria University study and subsequently several factors were omitted to reflect the different life circumstances of mature students.

Why leave?

What were the factors that played a part in decisions to withdraw? Students were given an opportunity to indicate, from a range of issues, those that had an influence on their decision. Research indicates that rarely is there only one reason for withdrawing. Rather it is a combination of factors that leads to the decision.[6]

Only nine of the mature students, all women, indicated that coping with study was a contributing factor to their withdrawal –

I should have done a pre-university course to gain skills in essay writing, research, computer skills etc.

I struggled to develop a regular study programme (much the same when a full-time student)

The most important factor for mature students who withdrew from study was the limited amount of time they had available for university because of their other commitments. In the 40-plus postal survey, 74% indicated that availability of time was a barrier to study for them. This is hardly surprising given their stage of life and the competing demands on their time. For a number of these mature students the pressures created by paid employment made it impossible to fit in some sort of life as well as study – so study went.

Work commitments took over. University study is secondary to work and family. Fitted it in around these two things. A young staff member would not take these things into account and because I am dealing with people at the bottom of the heap all the time, this did not necessarily fit in with academic thinking.

I started a new full-time position in April. This along with caring for a parent who has dementia made the workload greater than I could manage.

Work commitments are a priority and I couldn't handle the extra pressure.

At my workplace, staff are entitled to take some time for study but its just too challenging to do because of the workload. Also I found that other staff who were not studying can feel resentful if I do try to use this study time.

As can be seen in Table 10.1 below, time pressures were paramount for older students and were cited twice as often as any other reason. While younger students also face competing time pressures only 9% indicated limited time for university was a factor in withdrawing.

Table 10.1: Main Reasons for withdrawing from Victoria University

40-plus Women	%	40-plus Men	%
Limited time	65	Limited time	50
Personal/family problems	38	Left for something more important	22
Financial	24	Financial	22
Medical	24	Poor quality teaching	22
Younger women		**Younger men**	
University environment did not suit me	33	Left for something more important to me	35
The course does not suit my career choice	26	The course does not suit my career choice	30
Discovered I did not like the course	28	Financial problems	26
Not committed enough to study	26		

The older women and men students generally had very similar reasons for their withdrawal from study. But there were quite marked gender differences among the younger students.

Across the different studies, around a quarter of the students who had withdrawn did so because they had decided that there was something more important for them to do at this stage rather than be at university.

40-plus Victoria students   22%
Younger Victoria students   28%
Curtin students   24%

There is a gender difference. Male students were more likely than female students to leave the university for something that was more important to them. This suggests the possibility that males are being proactive, and making a positive decision to withdraw rather than reacting to an adverse situation by withdrawing from it. As one mature man commented –

> I partly achieved each of my goals; developed research skills, explored professional interests, reached point of diminishing returns (i.e. too much hassle, life is too short, there are plenty of other things I can do).

On the other hand an older woman student said –

> I asked myself – what the hell am I doing this for?

Employment was a major consideration as were opportunities for study in different settings. These are comments from older students –

> I want to concentrate on doing the job well next year.

> I was offered the opportunity for overseas study in [a foreign language] during the break so decided to take it and withdraw from Victoria University.

> We decided to travel to Europe and the UK for three months.

Lack of commitment to or interest in their subject areas was one of the themes identified by Yorke, indicating probable withdrawal. Younger women students who had withdrawn echoed this sentiment and students who were continuing with their studies identified the importance of their own motivation as a key to success. This was not an issue for 40-plus students with only 9% indicating a lack of commitment or lack of interest as factor in their decision to withdraw.

However, nearly 50% of the younger students surveyed at the end of their first year had strongly agreed or agreed with the statement that, 'I haven't felt motivated to study lately.' This then became a major area of concern for those younger students who had left. Nearly a quarter felt that they were not committed enough to study. This was likely to be more of a problem for the women (26%) compared with the men (17%) and particularly for the women under 20 years of age (28%). These are much higher than the percentages found at Curtin and reflect a greater gender imbalance. Again this difference may well be related to the different times of the year that students were surveyed with the students at Victoria University having had more time and experience of study to draw on. Some comments from the younger students illustrate this.

Wasn't sure what I wanted to be doing at this stage.

I didn't have any problems with the University. I didn't really know what I wanted to do and I didn't want to muck around being there.

Wasn't quite sure where it was leading me. Wasn't suiting me.

However, among the mature students surveyed, 23% indicated that personal confidence/motivation was a barrier to study. For most of this group, this was not the sort of problem that intensified and subsequently became a reason for withdrawing.

Closely related to motivation and commitment are other reasons for leaving, such as choosing the wrong programme. Again, this was more of an issue for the younger students who may not have had sufficient information or clarity of goals when they started. The course they were enrolled in did not suit the career choice of 28% of the younger students with this being somewhat more likely for males than females (30% compared with 26%) and similar to the results found at Curtin (24% compared with 18%).

The wrong time for me now – bad timing and bad choice.

In comparison only four older students (5%) found that the course they were enrolled in did not suit their career and four discovered they did not like the course after it began. In the postal survey, 88% of students aged 40-plus indicated that they were satisfied or very satisfied with their choice of courses. This suggests that they deliberated quite carefully before making their choices and were thus satisfied with the outcome.

The older students had higher expectations of the quality and helpfulness of university staff and in the postal survey showed that 78% were satisfied or very satisfied with their teaching. However, the juggling act required to fit study in around the other aspects of their life meant that mature students were less tolerant of deficiencies in course delivery. Twenty percent of the older students, compared with 11% of the younger students, indicated that poor quality teaching was a factor in their withdrawing. Nine percent of both the younger and the mature student group saw the unhelpfulness of staff contributing to them withdrawal.

> Individuality is not recognised by tutors. Classes are too big, no personalisation.

> I resented the significant amount of time wasted in dealing with administrative and academic requirements. I expected these requirements to be clearly and easily available (they were not).

Among the older students only four women, and no men, identified the university environment as a factor impacting on their decision to withdraw. This was the main reason given by withdrawing students in an English study[7] and was one of the major factors for the younger students. The following comments indicate some of the salient issues.

> Culture shock after private school education.

> Too much of a transition from work to study.

> Environment – I was a mature student at 23 years and neither a real first year nor an adult student.

The younger women were more likely to identify the university environment as a concern than the men (33% as against 17%). The environment was not an important factor in the Curtin study, possibly because the students interviewed there were early withdrawals and had not had time to establish what the environment was like. The older students at Victoria had a much wider range of experiences to draw on, having been in a variety of diverse circumstances over their lives. The university experience provided another example of a diverse environment that they were required to navigate. However, there were features of the environment that were remarked upon.

> If the environment and tutor were more friendly towards older students I could have stayed.

> The last recent study experience was relatively bleak.

This is not necessarily something that the university can address in any systematic way – rather it is up to the individual student. However, the university can act to improve the quality of the teaching and to make sure that the environment is not seen as alienating.

Some of the practical difficulties associated with attending lectures impacted on the decision to withdraw, as one older woman student indicated –

> Had there been car parking available it might have been easier to attend classes. It took an hour to get to class using the train and I went directly to work in the afternoon.

Parking and transport were noted as a barrier to study in the postal survey.

There has been a great deal of discussion over recent years about the cost of university study, particularly with regard to student loans and the burden of repayment. Although not necessarily the main reason that students find their time at university stressful, financial worries in combination with other factors, such as the need to be in paid employment and to balance the various components of their life, detract from the university experience. Research by Astin and Yorke et al has indicated that financial problems and high levels of indebtedness are major disincentives to further study. Issues around not wishing to get into debt have also been a factor with some groups of prospective students.

Seventy-five percent of students surveyed at the beginning of their first year at Victoria University in 1996 signalled that they thought finance would or could be a problem and by the end of the year 46% found that it had been. Besides reflecting the increasing costs of study, it also relates to the cost of living and mounting student debt. Financial problems were given as a factor contributing to their withdrawal by 24% of the younger students – 26% of the males and 23% of the females.

> I have to travel in from the Hutt by train each day so I am working for a year to be able to afford this ($60 per month in fares).

> Strictly financial reasons – saving to pay off current student loan.
> Plan to return but will still need a student loan to finance my study.

Financial problems also figured among the older students' decisions to withdraw – cited by 23% of those at Victoria and 24% of mature students at Curtin.

I thoroughly enjoyed the experience, made me realise that I enjoy study and will hope to return when I have the money.

There was a major gender difference among the older students when considering the influence of personal/family problems on the decision to withdraw. Twenty-two women (38%) indicated this was an issue compared with just two men (11%).

I needed to take time out. My husband travels a lot and we couldn't really cope.

It drove my wife mad. Too much. I did my Master's part-time when 30 – to do this again at 46 was too much for her.

Its very demanding to do *well* so, I decided to do other things like have family life and personal life instead. I miss it heaps.

Exhaustion! My daughter made the decision for me – she wants and needs time with me. Sometimes there is just not enough to go around!

Medical reasons for withdrawal also figures more prominently among the older women students (cited by 24%) than among their male counterparts (11%). These reasons are likely to be related to lack of time when trying to combine work, study and family life. A resultant high level of stress leaves these women vulnerable to both physical and emotional health problems.

Got very tired at times, trying to keep up work, spend time with family and get reading/essays in.

Having to combine so many part-time jobs with full-time study that something had to snap. In my case it was an assignment worth 40% and my health.

Health also deteriorated. Raised blood pressure due to stress.

There is conflict for women between education and the family role, as often they receive no practical support from partners, and in some cases hindrance.[8] As already indicated, mature students face a high level of competing demands for their time and in the end when something has to be abandoned university study tends to be the most expendable.

Extremely difficult which is why I withdrew. My work is more than full-time. I have a daughter with a serious spinal injury who is in chronic and I had three months this year to look after her and a partner who is brain damaged.

Husband resented my attempts to 'get an education'.

The impact of [a particular piece of work] was too great. The pressure of completing it over a short time impacted on our time and family life suffered

Personal and/or health problems were for both younger and older students, but they are likely to have a greater impact on the latter group because of the complexity of their life.

Future study plans

While around a third of the older respondents gave no indication of their future plans with regard to study, only one person definitely saw their withdrawal from Victoria University as the end of their higher education (Table 10.2). Most did not see this as a permanent withdrawal from higher education and nearly half wanted to return to the same course at some time in the future. This is a similar result to that found in the study of younger students.

Table 10.2: The future study plans of 40-plus withdrawing students

	Women		Men	
	No	%	No	%
Return to the same course later	27	47	10	56
Transfer to another university course	5	9	1	6
Study at another tertiary institution	7	12	1	6

However, as one older student pointed out, any return to study will be influenced by earlier experiences.

I have by no means found a satisfactory balance [between work, family and study] especially in times of difficulty. This fact will definitely influence my future intentions.

Conclusion

So where does this lead? In an era when it is acknowledged that attracting mature students to university, and retaining them, is important, universities need to consider the research findings and what may be done about them. The issues identified in the overseas literature and by the younger students in the Victoria study are echoed in the concerns voiced by the 40-plus students. In particular, students need to feel that their tertiary study is of value to them and they are achieving what they set out to accomplish, in an environment that is not seen as either alien or alienating. This is crucial for mature students. Unlike younger students, some of whom tend to 'drift' into tertiary study, mature students have made a deliberate choice to be at university and withdrawing is not a decision that is made lightly.

While it is a combination of factors that leads to withdrawing from study, the pre-eminent factor for the older students was time. This was an issue for three quarters of respondents to the 'Education in Mid and Later Life' postal survey and was a major problem for over half of those who withdrew. Trying to achieve a balance between study, paid employment and family responsibilities is not easy. It requires a high level of organisation to ensure that the older student is able to maintain the level of involvement they want in all aspects of their lives. The equilibrium can be upset by unexpected crises or extra demands which need to be somehow incorporated into a finite amount of time. When it came to the crunch, family and paid employment usually took precedence over study. Family, personal and health problems could thus be deciding factors for what was often a temporary withdrawal.

While the older students who withdrew had some concerns around the quality of the teaching, generally they were much less likely than their younger counterparts to have problems with motivation, the university environment and the relevance of the courses they had chosen. A level of maturity and experience in weighing up options clearly worked to their advantage and only a small number of withdrawing mature students indicated these were the areas that influenced them.

Finance was a problem for all withdrawing students. Older students were generally relying on a combination of sources of income during their study, and for those who withdrew it was clearly becoming too hard to manage. What may have seemed reasonable when planning for study became a difficult proposition in reality.

For the students who withdrew, their difficulties had reached a stage where the negative aspects of the university experience outweighed any benefits. However, this was not necessarily seen as permanent state of affairs. A majority indicated a future that involved study of some kind. Perhaps they would be in a better position when they returned because they had learnt from their previous experience. Demands on time can change as can the nature of personal and health problems. Continued study at some period in the future would then be a viable option for the older students – one they could enjoy and benefit from.

Notes

1 McInnis (1997).
2 Tinto (1987) (1995), Astin (1993), Yorke at el (1997).
3 McInnis et al (1995).
4 McInnis (1997).
5 Russell (2001).
6 Bourner et al (1991).
7 Ozga and Sukhnandan (1997).
8 Parr (2000).

11

CONCLUSION – COMMON THEMES AND POLICY POINTERS

Judith A Davey, Jenny Neale and Kay Morris Matthews

The work which led to this book arose very broadly from an interest in the implications of population ageing in New Zealand. But, more specifically, the research posed questions about why adults over forty years of age are taking up study opportunities and how educational institutions might better plan, promote, process and deliver courses of study to older students, given increasing numbers in this group and the possibility of further growth in the future, as pointed out in chapter one. Other factors which encouraged our interest in the topic included our personal experiences and enjoyment of teaching mature students at university and, for some of us, the fact that we have been mature university students ourselves.

The preceding chapters, covering the nine in-depth studies which arose from the postal survey of early 2000, illustrate considerable diversity among students aged 40 and over who were studying at Victoria University. They included people in midcareer as well as those nearing and in retirement; people for whom university, or any type of higher study, was a new experience and those engaged on their second, third or subsequent qualifications. The participants in the survey and subsequent interviews were studying for a wide range of qualifications in a variety of subjects. As the vignettes presented show, their personal experiences and backgrounds were equally rich in variety. In concluding the book, we try to identify some common themes and issues from the miscellany, drawing on the research as a whole and especially on material derived from four 'core' questions, which were included in all the follow-up interview schedules. These covered motives for coming to university, difficulties encountered in the process of study, and outcomes.

Motives for study

Why did these people come to university at this stage of their lives, when attitudes in society tend to suggest that education is something for the young? Many were driven by economic motives – to improve earning capacity, retain a job or find a new one. Others were studying for its own sake, for the joy of learning. There were some who wanted to do something for themselves, who wanted to set an example to their children and grandchildren and even a few who wanted to prove to their parents, former teachers, or even former partners, that they had been underestimated and undervalued. Two dominant purposes emerged across all the groups that were studied (including those who left without completing qualifications). These were work-related motives and those related to personal development/self-fulfilment. But there were different nuances within these categories. Study for professional or career development was usually seen in a positive light, reflecting an opportunity for choice as far as the individual student was concerned, and the potential for advancement.

> [My study was] related but an extension to my field of employment. A logical explainable extension to my career, yet subjects that pushed the boundaries of my knowledge and experience.

> The IT industry has now got a higher profile and there will be more jobs in this area in the future.

> My degree is based on my previous work in horticulture, in a way that adds to it. I have looked at a lot of jobs advertised which I would like to do and have tried to tailor my studies to achieve this goal.

> Initially when I started study the reason was to work in Europe. I recognised a 2nd language was required.

However, work-related study was sometimes seen more negatively, as a requirement to maintain a current position rather than to gain advancement, or sometimes akin to compulsory training, as the following comments illustrate –

> The four Master's papers I have undertaken were a compulsory requirement of my job. I could not have afforded them had they not been paid for my employer.

I didn't have a choice over the content studied.

This is the first time I've entered compulsory study. It is much less satisfying.

The course was a compulsory component of my job. There was no choice in what I have taken for the past two years. However, if I continue I now have a choice.

It seems that credentialism is a factor affecting many workers in midlife, including those who have lost their jobs, fuelled by lack of job security. Advanced qualifications are deemed essential to keep up with the pace of change, to illustrate continuing competence despite increasing age, and in particular are essential for senior or management roles. Many respondents saw further study almost as insurance against losing their jobs as they looked around and found that all their co-workers were graduates, or that younger workers, with glowing credentials, were breathing down their necks.

Women were as likely to express work-related purposes in their study as men and many approached their university studies with the knowledge they already had from nursing or teaching experience. This meant that the transition into university was not as difficult for them as it would have been had they undertaken completely new fields of study. Most of the women respondents had come from strongly female-dominated areas of work – teaching, nursing and office work. Many had had time out from paid work to rear families. Stereotypical gender expectations have loomed large in the life courses of women now past 40, as many of the previous chapters show.

Personal development motives were evident in the experience of many older students.

It was stimulating to be in the university environment studying, and in a sense competing against people less than half my age! (man)

I find lectures always interesting and on many occasions a wonderful mixture of serious food for thought and fun. (woman)

Where people had come to university study later in life, especially the early school leavers, personal development frequently led to increased self-confidence and self-belief, which gave them advantages in many areas of their lives. This helped them to cope with the stresses, and sometime traumas of adult life and, in many cases also had positive effects on work experiences. For the group of students aged over 60, university study was a way of keeping themselves active in retirement, but it also gave them considerable satisfaction and even joy, as well as fulfilling the need for structure and 'busyness'.

The mature Māori students saw the realisation of cultural goals being as important as those of employment or personal development. They saw themselves as working towards the common good rather than individual achievement. However, they found that whānau responsibilities, based on the principle of common good, took up a great deal of time and resulted in many older Māori students feeling very torn between their immediate and long-term commitments and goals.

Overcoming difficulties

A dominant theme emerging from this study and from others of adult students in different contexts and different countries is the need for older students to face and overcome barriers and difficulties if they are to remain at university and be successful. These challenges came in many forms, but they are familiar from the literature. Difficulties may be internal or external in origin. The study of early school leavers, of men studying full-time and cases from other chapters show the problems for people who had no family history of tertiary study and/or had not completed entry qualifications at school. These interviewees frequently experienced lack of support for intellectual aspirations from family, either early in life, or when they decided to undertake university study, or from colleagues. A surprising number of the 40-plus students had suffered trauma in their lives, either previous to or while they were studying, including marital breakdown, redundancy, deaths and suicide in their families, their own illness or that of people close to them. These not only distracted them from their study ambitions and added to time constraints, but also sometimes led to self-doubt and even depression.

Money to finance their study could also be a problem, if not for the majority, then certainly for groups of older students such as sole parents, those who had several dependants and people who were studying full-time.

> The financial outlay occurring at the same time I'm educating my two sons.

Struggled to work enough to survive financially.

While some students were being supported by their employers, others were relying on their own earning capacity, family support, savings and student loans. There was a clear difference between people in high-paid and relatively secure employment who were studying part-time and were under little financial pressure and people seeking to establish themselves in the labour market after a period of childcare, unemployment or redundancy. The latter continued in the hope that their enhanced qualifications would lead to better employment prospects.

People studying in midlife face quite different challenges to the traditional school leaver student. These challenges are inherent in the variety of roles which the midlife student must juggle – worker, parent, spouse, community member, student – and in the conflicting time demands which these produce. These issues play out differently for men and women. The special challenge for most older women at university, seen clearly in several of the studies, was to juggle the responsibilities of caring for families and keeping house alongside paid work (often full-time). Some women pointed to support from their families –

I really enjoy what I am doing and remain enthusiastic with equally enthusiastic support from all of my family.

My husband, son and [overseas] student all took responsibility for cooking, cleaning etc. which was a positive thing.

Where such support was not forthcoming, continuing study became difficult and the research produced many examples where lack of support led to withdrawal from study, marital break-up, or even both. On the other hand, in order to keep up paid work and study many men were reliant on the support of their partners to undertake the family caring work and keep the household going. Several clearly acknowledged this.

I have a very supportive and understanding wife without whose help I could not have completed this course. Work·was also very understanding and gave me time off to meet deadlines.

Making room for study involved advanced time management, tenacity and commitment. For some, in the end it became impossible to keep up with all the parts of their life – study, employment, and family

– and the only solution was to withdraw from university, at least in the interim. Those who did not have problems tended to be the men studying full-time who treated university in the same way that they had treated their employment, and those over 60 who were retired and saw study as something constructive to do with their time, an enjoyable way of keeping busy.

Outcomes

The older students in the Victoria University study had made choices about what to study based on interest, employment requirements and aspirations, or a combination of the two. They faced, and usually overcame, or at least coped with, a variety of challenges as they worked through their courses. The outcomes often differed from the original objectives and were mixed in their effects. People gained qualifications, which improved their intellectual/academic capability and career prospects but also increased confidence and self-esteem. Those who had experienced redundancy found that their self-confidence had improved regardless of whether they were able to subsequently move back into paid employment (of their choice) or not. Many women found that they were able to manage their complicated lives and also did well in their studies, often to their own surprise.

> One positive spin-off from this is that the new job my law studies has helped me secure will enable me to spend more time with my family.

People in retirement frequently took satisfaction from their degree achievements even if they were not going to use them in paid work. Early school leavers and Māori students stressed the example they were setting for their children and grandchildren. The irony of coming to a western institution to learn about their own culture and language had not escaped the Māori students.

For those who had left school with few or no qualifications, university study gave them the opportunity for further study, increased and enhanced career opportunities. It was these students more than others who reported having 'something to prove', particularly to parents, and particularly to fathers. Closely linked to feelings of self-worth and identity, both men and women emphasised the 'feel good' factor in completing a degree and the opportunity to 'do something for myself'.

The only thing I did it for was me. I've already got qualifications that will get me where I want to go in terms of work . . . I did not do it for that. I did if for purely selfish reasons – that was for me to know that I could do it. It enriched me intellectually, it certainly enriched me the way I carry out my job, it enriched my friendships that I developed – I met some wonderful people that I'm friends with now, there's so many things . . . it's such a positive experience all up.

Those who saw their study as forced considered that their life experience was not counted and getting 'a piece of paper' was more important than anything else in order to keep or advance in their employment. Others who may have started grudgingly took the opportunity offered and thrived. Initial resentment and the juggling act required to fit study into their lives became less significant.

It's very difficult and tests your relationships at times. At times also you were stressed to the limit but as you achieved your goals it could be euphoric. It has been worth it but if I had been aware of what was involved at the outset I probably wouldn't have started.

Students in this study pointed to the value of being able to reflect on theory and practice. They saw postgraduate study as rather more than just upskilling in a narrow vocational training sense.

Having a Master's degree has given me confidence, and a vast reservoir of research to draw on to advance educational debate with people. As a credential with my work, it's absolutely critical, working with companies and large organisations. The first thing they want to know is whether you've actually got the credibility to be doing the kinds of things that you are doing . . . It opens doors and it was a very fulfilling thing for me personally.

The outcomes illustrated in the nine studies clearly demonstrate the value of university study in mid and later life. What then can be done to encourage people in this endeavour and to support them once them embark upon their learning adventure?

Policy implications

At the institutional level
Students aged 40 and over are more likely to be taking postgraduate

qualifications than the student body as a whole and it is postgraduates in particular who find that the university is not meeting their needs. Ever aware of the thousands of dollars they pay for a Master's degree or postgraduate diploma, older students, who are often also members of professions, are rightly demanding better service and facilities. It is here that the university and its constituent schools need to implement changes. For example, responses to initial study queries are crucial, as the following example, from first-time university student in her 40s illustrates.

> It was the initial response of being with her . . . she made me feel *so* welcome, so knowledgeable . . . treated my professionalism with respect, that I felt and was very aware that I could go to her, even if I didn't have her as a lecturer. She would be available, and she would talk things through with me . . . Now, that to me was very important. I remember thinking if someone had been abrupt, I would not have carried on.

Whilst postgraduate programme directors, administrative staff and postgraduate student groups all provide advice and support, more practical measures, aimed at older students, are called for. These might include a designated staff member in each school with pastoral responsibility for mature students – an academic with time clearly earmarked for academic queries, mentoring, coordination of study/reading groups, as well as social activities. The teacher-students especially emphasised the need for someone who can be contacted to answer questions that arise, particularly related to research projects. For the university's part, taking the concerns of older students more seriously by facilitating access to staff outside the usual 9am–5pm hours would enhance the learning experiences which they offer.

Another way in which the university could promote itself as an attractive provider of postgraduate programmes is to sharpen delivery of administrative and study support services. Full-time professionals who are also part-time students, have little time to waste. Some reconsideration of the processes and issues associated with obtaining student ID cards, accessing library resources (especially databases), updating computer skills are clearly called for. The provision of computer facilities, study space and accessible car parking needs improvement. Although the adult students in this study were generally attracted to face-to-face classroom-based delivery and enjoyed the interaction with other students, some of the obvious 'system' frustrations could be alleviated in different ways. For example, increased electronic delivery of administrative and library requirements as well as of course components could enhance the study experience of the adult part-time student. Whilst these difficulties are shared with all postgraduate students, particularly those who are new to a campus, the provision of services in hours outside of the norm would greatly assist the growing and significant part-time student body. However, universities are addressing improved delivery of a range of services and curriculum to students at the current time. This issue was emphasised in the 'Tertiary Education Strategy 2002/7'. A recommendation makes it clear that tertiary institutions must take into account 'increased responsiveness to the needs of, and wider access for, learners'.[1] The accompanying text has particular significance for adult learners at university.

> In a knowledge society all New Zealanders will require enhanced access to relevant education and training (and career and academic advice and guidance) throughout their lives . . . This creates a challenge for providers to deliver learning in innovative ways that meet the diverse needs of learners. This will require a shift to more diverse and interconnected learning pathways.[2]

At central government level

Any consideration of lifelong learning must take account of the ways in which older students move into and out of study. While some of those included in this study followed traditional paths, this was not always the case. To meet the challenges of lifelong learning and the 'Learning Society', the tertiary system must retain its flexibility so that people can commence or resume study throughout their lifetimes. Measures such as incentive allowances connected to university fee payments and provisions for study leave during working careers could be considered in the policy debate.

The suggestion, by the Tertiary Education Advisory Committee in 2001, that open entry to university for those over the age of 21 be removed, is of particular concern. Such a policy would have serious implications for both mature students and universities. Firstly, it would curtail opportunities for prospective students who are older; who can benefit from study and who often go on to develop enhanced and secure positions in paid work. From the wider policy point of view, people should be encouraged to prolong their working careers, reducing dependence on the state and premature retirement. Secondly, mature students add to the richness of the academic learning experience by contributing their wider experience and often lifting the breadth of discussion and insights for classes as a whole. Finally, such a shortsighted measure would erode student numbers significantly, as shown in the circumstances at Victoria University (outlined in chapter one). At Whare Wananga, where large numbers of mature Māori students are admitted under open entry policies, the result would be disastrous. Indeed, such a policy direction runs counter to the vision expressed in the New Zealand 'Tertiary Education Strategy 2002/7' where institutions are called upon 'to be more cognisant of, and more responsive to Māori learners with particular needs and aspirations such as Māori women and older learners returning to education'.[3]

In the policy context, we conclude that lifelong education and attendance at university should be promoted as a viable option for people of all ages and as a way of assisting people to cope in a changing society. Older students demonstrate the value of tertiary study to their immediate family and friends and also broaden the perspectives of the younger students with whom they interact. If open entry to university is restricted, then the objectives of the 'Learning Society' will be compromised. This will not only affect people now in midlife. Today's younger students will also be affected in the longer run. In a changing world of employment, the young students of today are increasingly likely to return to the university later in their lives, seeking higher qualifications and retraining associated with their jobs. As older students they too will have to confront the roller coaster world of combining study with paid work and/or parenting. Policy settings need to consider the needs not only of this generation of older students, but also oncoming cohorts. In addition, a wide range of policies needs to be considered. It is not only education policy, but also policies related to employment, family support, income maintenance and ageing that are relevant. All these have the potential to either encourage older students returning to study or to place barriers in their path.

The last words in this book should go to the older students who made possible this research. Their participation, enthusiasm and interest continue to inspire us.

> The study was rejuvenating in so many ways . . . The world is changing so fast and one way of coping with change, let's face it, you are either going to cope with the change or you are going to fall behind desperately. The longer you leave it the more you are going to fall behind.

Notes

1 Ministry of Education (2002) 'Tertiary Education Strategy 2002/7'. Wellington p.16.
2 Ibid, p.18.
3 Ibid, p.30.

BIBLIOGRAPHY

Andrews, M. (1999). The seductiveness of agelessness. *Ageing and Society,* 19, 301–18.

Arthur, M., Inkson, K. and Pringle, J. (1999). *The new careers: Individual action and economic change.* London: Sage.

Arthur, M. and Rousseau, D. (eds) (1996). *The boundaryless career: A new employment principle for a new organisational era.* Oxford: Oxford University Press.

Astin, A. (1993). *What Matters in College.* Jossey-Bass, San Francisco.

Atchley, Robert C. (1989). A Continuity Theory of Normal Aging, *The Gerontologist,* 29, 2, 183–90.

Benn, R., Elliott, J. and Whaley, P. (1998). Introduction: Women and continuing education – where are we now?, in Benn, R., Elliott, J. and Whaley, P. (eds), *Educating Rita and her sisters: Women and continuing education,* 1–5. London: NIACE (The National Organisation for Adult Learning).

Biggs, S. (1997). Choosing not to be old? Masks, bodies and identity management in later life. *Ageing and Society,* 17, 553–70.

Blackie, S.A.H. (2001) *Women, Work, Study and Health: The experiences of nurses engaged in paid work and further education.* Unpublished MPhil thesis, Massey University, Palmerston North, NZ.

Bonnie Dewart, D.C. (15/10/1997). Mature Advice. *New Zealand Education Review.*

Bourner,T., Hamed, M., Barnett, R. and Reynolds, A. (1988). *Students on CNAA's part-time first-degree courses.* London: Council for National Academic Awards.

Bourner,T., Reynolds, A., Hamed, M. and Barnett, R. (1991). *Part-time Students and their Experience of Higher Education.* Buckingham, The Society for Research into Higher Education & Open University Press.

Browne, C. (ed) (1998). *Women, feminism and aging.* New York: Springer.

Burton, C. (1992). Merit and gender: Organizations and the mobilization of masculine bias, in Mills A. and Tancred P. (eds). *Gendering organizational analysis,* 185–96. Newbury Park, CA: Sage.

Butler, J. (1990). *Gender Trouble: Feminism and the Subversion of Identity,* Routledge, London.

Butler, J. (2000). Appearances aside. *Californian Law Review,* 88(1), 55–63.

Carpenter, H. (1971). *An approved system of nursing education for New Zealand.* Department of Health, Wellington.

Curnow, B., Fox, J. and Blass, E. (1994). *Third age careers.* London: Gower.

Davey, Judith (2001). *Going for it!: Older students at Victoria University of Wellington.* Victoria University of Wellington.

Dehler, G., Welsh, A. and Lewis, M. (2001).

Critical pedagogy in the 'new paradigm'. *Management Learning*, 32 (4), 493–511.

Doward, J. and Rigby, R. (2000, March). How to ageproof your career. *Management Today*, 56–7.

Doyal, L. (1995). *What Makes Women Sick: Gender and the Political Economy of Health*. London: Macmillan.

Dunstall, G. (1981). The Social Pattern, in W.H. Oliver (ed), *The Oxford History of New Zealand* (396–429). Wellington, New Zealand: Oxford University Press.

Durie, M. (1998). *Te Mana, Te Kawanatanga – The Politics of Māori Self Determination*. Auckland, Oxford University Press, 75–9.

Durie, M.H., Black, T.E., Christensen, J., Durie, A.E., Fitzgerald, E., Taiapa, J.T., Tinirau, E., Apatu, J. (1996). *Māori Profiles: An Integrated Approach to Policy and Planning*. Te Hoe Nuku Roa, the Department of Māori Studies, Massey University 7.6.

Dyer, S. and Humphries, M. (1999). 'Managing people through the concept of career', *From the Edge: Management Beyond... Australia and New Zealand Academy of Management (ANZAM)*, Hobart, Tasmania, 1–4 December.

Education in Mid and later Life Research Team (2000). 'Research Report prepared for Te Ripowai Higgins', Wellington, Victoria University of Wellington

Edwards, Rosalind (1993). *Mature Women Students: Separating or Connecting Family and Education*. London: Taylor and Francis.

Ekerdt, David J. (1986). The Busy Ethic: Moral Continuity between work and retirement, *The Gerontologist* Vol 26, No 3, 239–44.

Equal Employment Opportunities Trust. (2000). *Recruiting Talent: A research report*. Wellington: Equal Employment Opportunities Trust.

Gibson, H. (2000). It keeps us young. *Ageing and Society*, 20, 773–9.

Graham, B. (1989). *Older Graduates and employment. A report of the sub-committee on the employment and training of older graduates*. Association of Graduate Careers Advisory Service.

Hareven, Tamara K. and Adams, Kathleen J. (1982). Ageing and Life Course Transitions: An Interdisciplinary Perspective. London and New York: Tavistock.

Henderson, M. (2002, Jan. 13). The premature ageing of the job market. *Sunday Star Times*, C2.

Henderson, R. (2001/12/22,). Job seekers in their 30s hit by ageism-survey. *The Dominion*, 3.

James, D. (1995). 'Mature Students in Higher Education: beyond a species approach', *British Journal of Sociology of Education*, Vol.16, No.4, 451–66.

Jerrome, Dorothy (1994). Time, Change and Continuity in Family life. *Ageing and Society*, 14, 1–27

Kirkwood, T. (2001). *Making Choices. The End of Age, Reith Lectures, 2001*, BBC Radio 4. [Online] website

Leonard, M. (1994). 'Transforming the Household: Mature Women Students and access to higher education' in Davies, S., Lubelska, C. and Quinn, J. (eds). *Changing the Subject: women in higher education*, London: Taylor and Francis.

Lucas, R. (2000). Scrapheap mentality damages businesses. *Professional Engineering*, 13 (18), 26–7.

Lumby, J. (2001). *Who cares? The changing health care system*. Allen & Unwin, NSW, Australia.

McGregor, J. (2001). *Employment of the Older Worker: Helping Build a Better Workplace*. Palmerston North: Massey University.

McGregor, J., and Grey, L. (2001). *Mature job-seekers in New Zealand*. Palmerston North: Massey University.

McGregor, J., Thomson, M. and Dewe, P. (1994). *Women in Management in New Zealand: A Benchmark Survey.*

(Massey University). Women in Management Series, Paper 19, University of Western Sydney.

McInnis C., James, R. and McNaught, C. (1995). *First Year on Campus Diversity in the initial experiences of Australian Undergraduate.* Centre for the Study of Higher Education University of Melbourne, Melbourne.

Manawatu Evening Standard (19/1/2002). 'High Māori dropout rate probed' (www.stuff.co.nz/inl/index/0,1008, 1074185a11,FF.html).

Mavin, S. and Bryans, P. (1999). Gender on the agenda in management education? *Women in Management Review,* 14 (3), 99–104.

Middleton, S. (1987). Schooling and radicalisation: life histories of New Zealand feminist teachers. *British Journal of the Sociology of Education* 8(2):169–89.

Middleton, S. (1993). *Educating Feminists: Life Histories and Pedagogy.* New York: Teachers College Press.

Middleton, S. and May, H. (1997). *Teachers Talk Teaching 1915–1995.* Palmerston North: The Dunmore Press, 10.

Middleton, S. and Weiler, K. (1999). *Telling Women's Lives: Narrative Inquiries in the History of Women's Education.* Buckingham: Open University Press.

Midwinter, Eric (1998). 'Age and education', in Bernard, M. and Phillips, J., *The social policy of old age,* London, 40–55.

Ministry of Education (2001). 'Tertiary Education Statistics by Universities' (as supplied by the MOE to the Research Team).

Ministry of Social Development (2001). *Positive Ageing in New Zealand: diversity, participation and change. Status Report* 2001, Wellington.

Moses, B. (2001, 3 Feb.). Your destiny is in your own hands. *Management First.*

Ozga, J. and Sukhnandan, L. (1997). 'Undergraduate Non-Completion' in *Undergraduate non-completion in higher education in England.* Higher Education Funding Council for England December 97/29 Bristol.

Paterson, K. (1997). *The X-Factor: Finding Inner Courage.* Auckland: Penguin Books (NZ) Ltd.

Peters, T. (1999). *The brand you 50: Fifty ways to transform yourself from an 'employee' into a brand . . .* New York: Knopf.

Phillips, Judith (1998). *The social policy of old age: moving into the 21st century.* Centre for Policy on Ageing, London.

Pifer, Alan and Bronte, Lydia (1986). *Our Aging Society Paradox and Promise.* New York, Norton.

Pringle, J.K. and Mallon, M. (2001). Limits to the boundaryless career odyssey. Paper presented at *The Odyssesy of Organizing: The 17th European Group for Organizational Studies (EGOS) Colloquium,* Lyon, France.

Prison Review Committee (1989). *Te Ara Hou: The New Way.* Wellington, New Zealand: Ministerial Committee of Inquiry into the Prison System.

Redding, Nancy P., Dowling, W. D. (1992). Rites of Passage Among Women Reentering Higher Education. *Adult Education Quarterly,* 42(4).

Rendell, H. (1992). *Age Discrimination and Equal Employment Opportunities: A Review of the Literature.* Wellington: New Zealand State Services Commission.

Richardson, J. (1995). 'Mature Students in Higher Education:II. An Investigation of approaches to studying and academic performance', *Studies in Higher Education.* Vol.20, No.1, 5–17.

Russell, Ben (2001). Ben Russell in London, *NZ Education Review,* 12 January, 6.

Sargant, N., Fields, J., Hywell, F., Schuller, T., Tuckett, A. (1997). *The Learning Divide: A Report of the Findings of a UK-wide Survey on Adult Participation and Learning.* Leicester, England: National Institute for Adult Continuing Education.

Schuller, T., Raffe, D., Morgan-Klein and Clark,I. (1999). *Part-Time Higher Education: Policy, Practice and*

Experience. London: Jessica Kingsley (Higher Education Policy Series).

Sparrow, M. (1999). *Midwinter spring: Smart business and older workers.: The research: Labour Market demographics Survey* 1999. Auckland: EEO Trust.

Statistics New Zealand (1996). Census Employment and Unemployment (Online). http://www.stats.govt.nz/domino/external/PASFull/PASFull.nsf

Statistics New Zealand (2001). *Births and Deaths.* Year ending September 2001. http://www.stats.govt.nz.

Steinhauser, S. (1998, July). Age bias: Is your corporate culture in need of an overhaul? *HRMagazine*, 86–91.

Still, L. and Timms, W. (1998). Career barriers and the older woman manager. *Women in Management Review,* 13, 143–55.

Stuller, J. (2000). Ready for the other millennium time bomb? *Chief Executive,* 48–54.

Taylor, P. and Walker, A. (1998). Employers and older workers: Attitudes and employment practices. *Ageing and Society,* 18, 641–58.

Te Puni Kōkiri (2000). *Progress Towards Closing Social and Economic Gaps Between Māori and Non-Māori – a Report to the Minister of Māori Affairs.* Wellington.

Te Puni Kōkiri (2001). *Te Māori i ngā Rohe – Māori Regional Diversity.* Wellington.

Tertiary Education Advisory Commission. (2001). *Shaping the Funding Framework, Fourth Report of the Tertiary Education Advisory Commission* (4). Wellington, New Zealand: Ministry of Education.

Thomson, D. (2001). *Employment of the Middle-aged.* Presented at Supersummit, 21 May, Wellington.

Thompson, L. (1997). *Education Graduates' Post-Degree Learning Needs Study.* University of Regina:

Saskatchewan Instructional Development and Research Unit. Research Report No 18.

Tinto, V. (1987). *Leaving College.* University of Chicago Press, Chicago and London.

Tinto, V. (1995). *Learning Communities and Education in the First Year Experience* presented at the Inaugural Pacific Rim First Year Experience Conference, Brisbane.

Tong, R. (1989). *Feminist Thought.* Colorado, U.S.A: Westview Press.

Turner, Mike and Bash, Leslie (1999). *Sharing Expertise in Teacher Education.* London: Cassell.

Weedon, C. (1987). *Feminist practice & poststructuralist theory.* London: Basil Blackwell.

White, J. (1999). *Midwinter spring: Smart business and older workers.: New Zealand guide to best practice for employers in an ageing population.* Auckland: EEO Trust.

Witz, A. (1994). The Challenge of Nursing, in Gabe, J., Kellehear, D. and Williams, G. (eds). *Challenging Medicine.* Routledge: London: 23–45.

Yorke M. (1999). *Leaving early: non-completion in higher education.* Falmer London.

Yorke, M., et al (1997). 'Undergraduate Non-Completion in England' in *Under-graduate non-completion in higher education in England.* Higher Education Funding Council for England December 97/29 Bristol.

Young, Michael and Schuller, Tom (1991). *Life after Work; The arrival of the Ageless Society.* London: Harper Collins.

Wilson, Fiona (1997). 'The Construction of Paradox?: One Case Study of Mature Students in Higher Education'. *Higher Education Quarterly,* Vol.51, No.4, 347–66.